Walk In The Light

R.D. Ginther

Published by K.A.Edwards, 2021.

WALK IN THE LIGHT

First edition. January 26, 2021.

Copyright © 2021 R.D. Ginther.

ISBN: 979-8224652303

Written by R.D. Ginther.

Also by R.D. Ginther

Becca The Viking & The Heavenly Runes
Becca The Viking & The Heavenly Runes Book 1, Voyage to Lindisfarne
BeccaThe Viking & The Heavenly Runes Book 2 Voyage To Aachen
Becca The Viking & The Heavenly Runes Book 3, Voyage To The Holy Land
Becca The Viking & The Heavenly Runes Book 4 The Voyage Home

RetroStar Chronicles
Anno Stellae 1912
Vision From Space
Anno Stellae 1918
Anno Stellae 1939
Anno Stellae 1967
AnnoStellae 1969
Anno Stellae 1985 & Anno Stellae 1986
Anno Stellae 1987 & Anno Stellae 1994
Anno Stellae 1996 & Anno Stellae 2024
Anno Stellae 2113, Anno Stellae 2145, Anno Stellae 2146, Anno Stellae 2155, Anno Stellae 2165
Anno Stellae 2170
Anno Stellae 2171, Anno Stellae 2251

Anno Stellae 2382, Anno Stellae 2390-91, Anno Stellae 2392
Anno Stellae 2415, Anno Stellae 2433, Anno Stellae 2444
Ano Stellae 2457
Anno Stellae 2456, Anno Stellae 2460, Anno Stellae 4130, Anno
Stellae 4133, Anno Stellae 4146
Chronicle 39 Anno Stellae 5918, Chronicle 40 Anno Stellae 5920,
Chronicle 41 Anno Stellae 5923
Chronicle 42
Chronicle 43, Chronicle 44
Chronicle 45, Chronicle 46
Chronicle 47
Chronicle 48, Chronicle 49, Chronicle 50
Anno Stellae 6700, Anno Stellae 7074, Anno Stellae 7504, Anno
Stellae 7506
Chronicle 55 Anno Stellae 7537, Chronicle 56 Anno Stellae 8033,
Chronicle 57 Anno Stellae 8507
Chronicle 58 Anno Stellae 8732, Chronicle 59 Anno Stellae 10,272
Chronicle 60, Anno Stellae 10,682; Chronicle 61, Anno Stellae
10,999
Chronicle 62
Chronicle Of The Knights Of Axes Of Honor
Anno Stellae 2393
Anno Stellae 4148, Anno Stellae 4149, Anno Stellae 4150, Anno
Stellae 5909, Anno Stellae 5913

Standalone
Walk In The Light
Becca The Viking & The Heavenly Runebook Book 5
The Great Divide
Victorian Christmas Ballads

Table of Contents

R.D. Ginther's Bio

On my websites since 1997 and in earlier writings, I have one or more writings relating to my dad's death which occurred when I was five years old. It was a quest of mine early on to resolve the problem of a long-lived mystery and spiritual conundrum, which produced existential daily damage and challenges, harming my chances to survive and thrive.

My responses to cope with the many-headed hydra were in many ways self-defeating. I struggled in the dark, not knowing what exactly I was seeking that would explain the death of my father in terms of God's will and sovereignty. The explanation was the missing piece of a giant puzzle, deliberately withheld by my mother, as it turned out, and withheld for a GOOD reason.

I was finally released, it was sort of like opening Pandora's box. I got no end of difficulties, troubles, hurtful rejection and actual rebuffs from people, but it was also glorious, I saw clearly WHY my father died at the age of 42. He was full of vigorous manhood and my young, uncle died with him in the crash of the plane on a fox hunting trip.

It was the Divine Weaver, Almighty God, flipping the tapestry of life over at a perfect moment in my life, so I could see His magnificent and astounding pattern of His redemptive purpose. That cosmic and personal WHY I discovered instead of a former tangle of dark threads on the other side, animated me to write to tell the world what a glorious, redeeming Messiah and Father and Spirit is God over all that exists. I cannot keep it to myself! And it is too big a blessing for me to keep.

I am wholly convinced the Lord intended for me to share it as widely as possible to help others find such a God, so was I created and purposed for that task? God knows, but I am determined that He should receive all glory for His marvelous dealings to the day He takes me away.

Preface by R.D. Ginther

We have all heard the code word "Reset" by now. But what does a global society in reset mode mean? What does it actually entail? Is it a fast-track to Socialism and even full-blown Communism? Is it a government (the Big Brother tyranny that George Orwell envisioned in his nightmare book, 1984) of the most intrusive and despotic kind? How will ordinary people be impacted and how will life change for them, and us?

Ilie (Elijah) Coroama's life story is featured in the text and audio book formats, called "Walk in the Light," by R.D. Ginther. It exposes highly revealing and significant clues as to what that global reset really is, and what it will soon come to mean to us in the West and elsewhere. This book could not come at a better time than 2021.Fasten your seat belt, as this ride into the Orwellian world of Coroama's escape is truly a fast-track revelation of a global reset. In other words, we are shown the ordeals, challenges, hazards and threats to his life growing up in Romania. From 1948 and onward, there was a Communist-imposed regime which regulated every aspect of Romanian life in a brutal, police-state dedicated to Marxism, Lenin and Stalin.

If you are curious in the least as to what a global reset could mean and how it could radically change your life, then this true account will open your eyes to the reality of this reset hopefully before it takes control of any society and any nation.

Secondly, and this is more significant, Elijah's account shows how he and his wife Aurica, confronts the Communist state that was seeking to eradicate Christianity from Romania. It had hoped to turn them all into fear-shackled, mindless puppets, whose strings were being pulled by Soviet puppet masters in the Kremlin.

Being enslaved and impoverished, despite the grinding hard work and owning virtually nothing, the Coroamas kept faith in God alive. They had no real hope of advancement or gaining a better life for themselves and their children but God kept them alive and able to fight back and do the impossible. He helped them to defeat their arch enemies, time after time, and ultimately securing their freedom and a much better life in America.

The cost to the Coroamas was great, but the rewards were much greater. The whole journey was one of faith, learning how to trust God with each step of the way forward and to follow His leading. They learnt not turn aside for anything less, especially the "wisdom" of others which urged resignation, defeat and the invincibility of the state. They also had to battle their own discouragement, pain and weariness, during the many lengthy years of preparing for their deliverance from bondage in Romania.

Can we too gain some knowledge from their experience for our current time? Just in case the global reset replicates the same conditions, or worse, that terrorized, economically drained and subjugated Romania in the Soviet Empire era? You be the judge. This small book contains enormous worth if you give it a read. It is the kind of true account that you may well find impossible to put down, reading it through in one sitting.

It is your choice after all. Stay where you are, do nothing but what everyone else is doing, and take whatever is coming down the pike from the global reset and the forces propelling it. Or...do something different that will give you a much better pay-off, like believing and trusting in the heavenly Father for your deliverance and protection.

Step into the world of Romania under Communist Soviet surveillance and oppression. Keep in mind that this could well be what a global reset will bring to you in your neighborhood sooner than you expect. Then maybe you will find some vital, life-preserving tools that will help you survive this beast system, that masquerades as a caring and compassionate government. Yet, it will lay chains on you and drag you, where no human being would ever care to go.

Yes, the good news is that ordinary people can survive the beast system that George Orwell described to a "T" for "Terrible", and with a sense of humor intact. Elijah and Aurica proved it! But it will take faith to accomplish the impossible. Without faith, you will be trapped in circumstances you cannot change or overcome in the coming World of Reset. Yet it is overcoming by faith that can be grown in ordinary, daily lives. You are not born with this faith and neither does it drop miraculously from heaven.

Anyone who is on the level or sincere can learn to "Walk in the Light." If you are not a champion now, you can become one. All it takes is simple trust in God, believing His promises in the Bible, and a willing, yielding heart. With people such as you and me, God Almighty, who divided the Red Sea so that the Israelites could pass through on dry land, wants to do the impossible for us today. Let's not just merely resist but conquer this global reset His way and gain the glorious life promised by Him to each of us, His overcomers!

R.D. Ginther, December 28th 2020, author of WALK IN THE LIGHT

Foreword
Charles M. Duke, Jr.
280 Lakeview
New Braunfels, Texas 78130
629-1005

During the summer of 1981, I had the privilege of speaking to a large Christian rally at the Olympic Stadium in West Berlin. The rally was a three-day event so throughout that time I had the opportunity to listen to other speakers. One of those speakers was Ilie (Elijah) Coroama. As I listened, Ilie told the most amazing and inspiring story of God's leading and deliverance of his family from oppression and persecution in Romania.

When Ilie concluded his testimony, the Lord spoke to my heart that I should meet Ilie and that God would use him in my life. This meeting was the beginning of a relationship that now is in its thirty-ninth year and one that grows deeper each day. I have come to know Ilie as a dear brother in Christ and as a humble and anointed man of God.

I have had the pleasure of ministering with Brother Ilie throughout Europe and the United States. Everywhere we go God uses him mightily in signs, wonders and miracles. Many times, he has been in our home and blessed us and our friends with words of exhortation and encouragement as God speaks to him in visions.

Brother Ilie serves the Lord with all his being. His life and character reflect the light of Jesus as he walks daily in the light. He has been an inspiration to me and I know you will be moved to commit your life to God as you read his thrilling story.

Charles M. Duke, Jr.
Apollo 16 Moon Mission Astronaut

"Ilie {Elijah} was the key link in an international ring of smugglers, through which many tons of Bibles and Christian literature found long awaited reception in the hands and hearts of thousands of Believers in need. The episodes contained in this book are just a small part of his experiences, many of which we are witnesses."

Paul and Marcelle Ermuluk
Eastwest Mission, Austria,
and Buenos Aires, Argentina

"PURPOSE OF APPEARANCE: To give his testimony. Elijah {Ilie} was a persecuted Romanian Christian who was supernaturally led to freedom...around May 1974. Elijah received a prophecy that on October 9th, 1974, he would depart and leave his family and Romania behind. Elijah knew that it was impossible to escape without the Lord's help because of the heavy security around the border. Around 6-8 PM on October 9the Elijah saw a ..."

Excerpt from the 700 Club Fact Sheet,
September 12th, 1984
Anaheim, California

Romanian History: A Retrospect
COMMUNIST ROMANIA—BEFORE THE OVERTHROW OF THE DICTATORSHIP

FOREIGN TOURISTS SNAP pictures of quaint mountain villages and priceless monastery art, returning afterwards to resorts built by the Romanian government, each equipped with a bowling alley, a rock band, and a strip of sandy beach that is off-limits to the Romanian people...

Bucharest the capital, full of fine, old buildings built before World War 1 but empty of cars, and everywhere somber-faced people waiting for hours in lines to buy what little food there is in a hungry land that once was Europe's breadbasket...

Vast collective farms, once the great hope of socialist agriculture, turning to weeds and thistles as the equipment rusts in the fields, the farm managers unable to secure parts to fix them...

Aged factories and industries, long out-of-date, spewing forth black, deadly toxins over the towns and farmlands and into the rivers, spreading ugliness, death, and sickness in a land renowned for great natural beauty...

Seeking God in their distress, thousands of Christian men and women meet late at night in homes to escape police raids, or assemble in the dark by rivers, in forests, risking three-year prison sentences and huge fines, in order to conduct baptisms...

A twelve-year old girl loses her parents to gunfire from guards at the border, and alone she drags her five-year old brother away...

Impoverished, hard-working Romanian youth turns to sympathetic visitors from the affluent Western countries and cross their wrists!

Elijah, a brave Christian man, is arrested by the KGB secret police, beaten and interrogated for hours, then days. His crime? Transporting Bibles to Romania's northern, Soviet-occupied province of Moldavia.

One day, he hopes and prays with his wife when they are together again, they will find a way to escape to freedom with their family.

This is the story of how Elijah, and two companions found a way where there was seemingly no way...

WHO AM I?
Elijah's Brief Bio

MY NAME IS ELIJAH. I WAS BORN OF A
GERMAN-DESCENT FATHER AND A JEWISH
MOTHER IN MY BELOVED HOMELAND OF ROMANIA.
I AM, BY GOD'S GRACE, A U.S. CITIZEN NOW, BUT HOW
CAN
I FORGET ROMANIA? MY HEART WOULD
SURELY STOP IF EVER THAT HAPPENED!
I WEEP FOR MY COUNTRY EVEN NOW—FOR
THE DESPAIR THAT STILL RULES IN SO MANY
HEARTS LONG OPPRESSED BY COMMUNISM
AND DECADES OF DICTATORSHIP.
BUT LET ME TELL YOU OF THIS LAND OF
GREAT BEAUTY AND GREAT TRAGEDY,
WHERE GOD BESTOWED RICH FAVOR TO US IN OUR
TERRIBLE DISTRESSES, AND
IN MY OWN LIFE SHOWED THAT
HE WHO PARTED THE RED SEA FOR THE
PEOPLE OF ISRAEL FLEEING MIGHTY PHARAOH
ALSO CARED FOR MY BELOVED WIFE AND CHILDREN,
AND ME...

Chapter 1: "The Lion's Mouth"

My name is Elijah. My year of birth, 1940, in Vicovul de los, Romania (Vicoudejos on the map, and on the northern border of the country), witnessed the piecemeal destruction of a free and prosperous country by Soviet Russia, Hungary and Bulgaria, while Nazi Germany stood by encouraging Romania's foes. Heart-broken Romanians rose up everywhere in mass demonstrations, but they could do nothing. The king fled the country leaving a five-year-old boy as a figurehead ruler. There was a sort of government, a pathetic puppet whose strings were pulled by Nazis in Berlin. The government allowed massacres of Jews by the fanatical "Iron Guard" and the plundering of the entire nation by its Nazi overlord. The country was plunged into a hopeless war. The puppet government, without the people's consent, went to war against Soviet Russia in World War II to win back formerly lost territories. Losing the war, Romania also lost its freedom (and parts of Moldavia (Moldovia) and Bucovina and all of Bessarabia).

My father lost his life in World War II somewhere in Soviet territory. Since he was a wealthy man, my father was purposely sent to the front line to be killed. Even in the early years the communists were exerting control over Romania. Today foreign tourists flock to Moldavia, but when I was a baby it knew the regimented thunder of invaders' boots. I was still in my mother's arms when she gathered up her family and a few belongings to flee the approaching Soviet Army. After burying some precious things underground in a nearby forest, Mother fled from our large house with her five small children. She took a cow, a pillow, and a bag of flour. Everything else was left to the Soviets. Later in life I returned to see only the house's foundation. Mother might have saved her strength rather than bury valuables in the ground. Many people did this when armies invaded Romania. But the Soviets set explosives in the forests. Those who returned for their treasures were blown up. Many people died that way, including some of Mother's relatives. Hearing of their deaths Mother never went back. She moved to another village called Dornesti, into a small house with a little land attached. We had a garden, geese, a cow, chickens and a few sheep. All the children had to work since Father was dead. The family's lumber mills had been taken away.

Though Jewish, Mother believed in Jesus. This is how she came to believe in Him. In 1932 she was terminally ill. Father had taken her to doctors and spent large sums of money, but her condition deteriorated. Finally, a doctor at the hospital told Father to take her home so she could die in her own bed. This was the custom in Romania, so that people could come and see the expiring person at home. As she lay dying in bed, Father came to a difficult decision. He could let her perish in misery before his eyes or seek out a man of God to pray for her healing. Though not believing in Jesus, he had heard of people who believed. Some experienced miraculous healings.

Learning of a man who prayed for the sick, Father implored him to come. A crowd gathered in the house to see Mother for the last time. No one had hope except for Father. God's man arrived and first spoke to the people. He told them of miracles God had performed. Then he went to Mother's bedside. She was in the worst stage. She could not swallow anything solid. She would take a sip of tea only now and then. The cancer had consumed her body, and appeared as a massive, red breast ulcer. Everyone considered her as good as dead.

As the man prayed, a light with the brightness of lightning began to shine on this cancer-stricken sufferer. When this powerful light shone on her, Mother sat straight up and began speaking in another language, worshipping God as her Healer and Deliverer.

Father was horrified, thinking she had lost her mind. The man continued to pray. She arose, getting out of bed without anyone's help. The moment Mother stood on her feet, the gathered mass of disease was supernaturally severed from her body and fell to the floor. There was utter chaos in the room. Screams! Shouts! People had seen the bright light, and now this! Some rushed to help Mother, while others ran out of the house in fear.

"Please leave her alone!" the man said. "God is healing her." Mother sank to her knees, still speaking in the heavenly tongue. A fresh dress was brought and put on her. Strength returned to her body. Her face was shining. She could eat food again. The news of this extraordinary healing and recovery exploded all over the community. Mother herself knew of twenty Jewish families who became believers in Jesus as Messiah, for they had come to the house to see her die and instead had seen the instant transformation with their own eyes. Father also believed in Jesus as his personal Savior.

Elsewhere, belief in Jesus swept Romania. "Crosses of Suffering" were given to those who believed in Moldavia, where long-ago monasteries, built churches set like jewels in the Carpathian Mountains. Church walls were covered with fresco paintings depicting Romanian folklore and Biblical stories that have kept their original colors for hundreds of years—which cannot be equaled by modern techniques. Amidst the art wonders great suffering for believers in Jesus erupted!

Persecution began in earnest when orthodox clergymen enlisted the powers of the State to smash the evangelical movement. Evangelical believers were thrown into filthy prison cells or slain outright. If they would recant and press their lips to an Orthodox icon, they were set free. Some people denied newfound faith. Many suffered imprisonment, torture, and death for Jesus.

My uncle later told us how he was plucked from a public execution of evangelicals, upon whom the death sentence had been decreed by the martial court in the regional capital, Cherno (later Chernovitz under Soviet occupation during World War II). He and a group of fellow believers were lined up waiting to be shot. The soldiers stood ready for the order to shoot. Given permission, the group sang in praise of the victorious name of Jesus. As the condemned group gave honor to Jesus, awaiting their deaths, two soldiers fell on their faces under the power of God. During this disruption, while they were still singing, a messenger was rapidly galloping toward the prison on a leathered horse. Just before the soldiers fired at the people, he raced into the compound. "Don't shoot them!" he shouted. The law had been thrown out!

The cruel sword of persecution that began to swing in 1935-1936 formally cut down its last victim in 1940. Communists infiltrating the government had succeeded in sweeping old laws off the books, inadvertently saving the lives of thousands of evangelical believers. Yet Mother's faith was strengthened in the years of ecclesiastical persecution. She and fellow believers were prepared for later hardships and renewed persecution under a new communist regime in 1947. Deaths of a son (my twin), her husband and numerous relatives and friends never shook her faith. I cannot forget the life we lived in the mountain village of old Moldavia. Today (1989) at age 85, Mother, with an unwavering faith in her Lord, continues to live in Dornesti in much the same humble circumstances that I knew in childhood.

Chapter 2: "True Riches"

Nazi Germany held Romania in an iron vise, squeezing all life from the nation until Soviet armies came to "liberate" us. Our national riches were vital to the war machines of both the Axis (German, Italy, and Japan) and Western Powers. Romania's oil installations, according to Churchill, were the "taproot of German might."

I was four years old when U.S. bombers attacked the refineries at Ploesti, north of the capital. In 27 minutes, the secret operation coded "Tidal Wave" was over. Three hundred airmen died and 57 bombers were destroyed in the heaviest anti-aircraft barrage in all Europe; but the "taproot" of Nazi Germany's war machine was in flames.

Yet Romania had suffered much more in the past from the German juggernaut. In World War I the Central Powers of Germany and Austro-Hungary invaded Romania when she chose to side with Britain and France in the conflict. For that Romania was attacked and was, because of her small army and isolated position, easy prey. Our sovereignty was almost snuffed out by the invading Germans by the time the Central Powers collapsed. Though Romania had been forced to sign an armistice with the invader, she was awarded much territory at the peace conference after the war because of her valiant stand. The nation nearly doubled in size, increased by territory mostly Romania in population.

My father was German, born in Romania, and my grandparents had business ventures in the old Austro-Hungarian Empire, so my family was not anti-German in sentiment. Neither was Romania against German culture, for Romania had a popular German-descent dynasty that went back to 1881, when King Karol of Germany's royal house of Hohenzollern-Sigmaringen was officially proclaimed king. The Coroama family owned mills and large estates in the country, which were run feudal-style, with many serfs and servants. They lived like other country gentry, enjoying the life style of the rich.

When cold winter weather had passed, stately houses throughout Romania sprang to life with festive gatherings amidst clipped green grass and formal gardens full of flowers. Keen to take part in gala balls were the Gypsies. Poplar-lined roads were full of caravans as they hurried to entertain the gentry with wonderful virtuosity on their violins. It was a common sight to see Gypsies in bedraggled, threadbare clothes, cavort and dance and make music, in bizarre contrast with their hosts in the dinner jackets and sequined gowns ordered from Paris. Such events paid the Gypsies well, so they were always available when such events were held.

But the Nazis stripped Romania to the bone, and the gentry were soon impoverished. By the time the communists were in power, Romania was not even a shadow of what it had been before the Second World War. Despite the loss of our family fortune, I tried to make the best of reduced circumstances, as only a little boy can. After school I loved to take friends and play "army." I was the captain. I dressed the part in some old bits and pieces of a uniform. Soldiering was a great game. We all loved parading about in formation and going on various military maneuvers. But soon the grim realities around us took playtime away.

I was twelve years old (1952), when my oldest brother and I saw two neighbors miraculously healed of cancer. I knew they were not believers in Christ as personal Lord and Savior as our mother was, so I was amazed. How could God heal people who cared nothing for Him, I wondered? It was then that I was struck in the heart, as by a lightning bolt, with the saving love and grace of God. At that moment my heart and life were surrendered to Jesus. So, we ran home to tell Mother the news, not only about the healing, but how Jesus had come and entered into our hearts.

Mother could share our joy. For Peter and me, the coming of Jesus Christ into our hearts meant life would never be the same. An older sister did not understand, however. Neither did some relatives. Most Romanians believed going to Orthodox services a few times a year was enough to make them Christians. My friends did not understand my experience and left me. Yet later, some returned and became joyful believers in Jesus. Though a mere boy, I started prayer meetings at home, inviting children and young people to come. But this was just the beginning of Christ's life in me. On becoming a believer in Jesus, I gave up my dreams of storing up earthly wealth and treasures.

My family had once known great wealth. But Christ, the Good Shepherd of Psalm 23, promises to take care of His children. I decided to trust Him alone for my needs. Perhaps the loss of the family fortune was for the best. Never could we build again on the foundation of the old life and the world. The Coroamas had found a new and greater Treasure in Jesus. Joining with fellow believers in Jesus, I witnessed of the Savior in poems and songs throughout Romania. Original poems of up to one hundred lines flowed from my heart. Everyone acknowledged that it was a gift of God. People wept when they heard poems glorifying the Savior pouring from a schoolboy.

But without Father life was hard. All five of us children worked however we could to support the family. From the earliest age I earned a few lei tending sheep and did farm work for people during school vacations. It required long hours of labor in order to survive. Our sandwich for lunch consisted of a lone piece of cheese. But Mother trained us well and loved us. She dressed us in clean clothes without the benefit of a modern washing machine.

At school the children training for the Young Communist League were privileged to wear bright, red scarves with their blue uniforms.

I felt, nevertheless, honored as a child of God. Though despised for my faith, and not acknowledged academically when my scholastic performance proved superior, I remembered the pain and humiliation the Savior suffered in this world:

> *O Lamb of God, please grant me strength*
> *To stand and suffer for your Name;*
> *How else may I fully know the length*
> *And depth and height of Love Who came?*

Chapter 3: "The Shepherd Boy"

When communism took complete control of Romania after World War II, the gold scepter and crown of Romanian sovereignty and freedom were crushed. The last king of Romania was exiled in 1947, and the country was proclaimed a communist state.

My boyhood slipped away as the nation was made a USSR satellite. In this overflowing breadbasket of East Europe, poverty swept plates bare throughout the land. Private ownership and bank accounts were abolished, as higher-priority steel mills were built and collective farms organized. Laws made it impossible to feed livestock. Farm people risked arrest. They had to drive starving cattle to government headquarters all over Romania and abandon them.

Romania is a land good for raising sheep. In 1956 when I was sixteen, I was a shepherd and learned about sheep first-hand. I thought often of Moses, who tended sheep for forty years. I also read Jacob's story. As I lay down on the ground to watch the flock and catch some rest, I could easily imagine Jacob fleeing in the wilderness. I could see him vainly attempting to sleep, for his hunter-brother, Esau, from whom he had stolen his birthright, might be lurking nearby, waiting to pounce upon him.

One day while tending the flock, an angel suddenly appeared to me. I fell to the ground. As it must have happened to Jacob, the angel gazed at me. His countenance was radiant, his clothing a glistening white, and he had bright, gleaming, golden hair. "Don't be afraid," he said reassuringly. "I came to see you because God has heard your prayers. Stand up!" It was true, as the angel said. All that summer I had been continually praying and seeking God. But struck dumb and helpless at the sight of the angel, I lay overwhelmed on the ground. "God wants to use you," the angel continued. "From a young age He chose you to be a leader of many people, a witness to multitudes in many nations."

I heard the angel's words, but I did not understand. There was no way a mere shepherd boy could imagine himself a witness to nations outside Romanian borders. The angel also said God would show His power and guide me in a mighty way, revealing new things. Then he left, leaving me trembling but filled with joy. I had seen God's power and divine reality. From that time, I trusted God more, becoming a stronger witness. He began to give me visions to encourage the faith of others.

I heard the angel's words, but I did not understand. There was no way a mere shepherd boy could imagine himself a witness to nations outside Romanian borders. The angel also said God would show His power and guide me in a mighty way, revealing new things. Then he left, leaving me trembling but filled with joy. I had seen God's power and divine reality.

"Son of Jacob, fear not!" God was saying to me through the angel's appearance. "I will be your God, and will protect and guide you wherever you go."

The God of Jacob and Bethel is still with us today and hears the cries of fearful, despairing hearts.

Chapter 4: "The Little Lamb"

In my teens I went to work in a clothing factory. I would return home late at night from the second shift. Usually Mother was waiting and had something ready for me to eat. One night, however, I stepped into the house and there was no one. The silence was not normal; I went into Mother's bedroom to see what had happened.

She was lying in bed. I spoke to her, but there was no answer. I saw that her face was ghastly white. I touched her, but she was cold and lifeless. Quickly, I ran to get help from relatives and neighbors. But before I reached the door, a Voice stopped me in my tracks: "Son, go back and pray for your mother right now!"

I knew my Shepherd's voice. I went back. Trembling, I took my Mother's hand. It was cold, dead and stiff. How long had she been lying like that, I wondered, grief stricken. Weeping as I prayed, I felt a warmth beginning to return to her hand. Then her left hand moved a little. She was coming back from death! Then I felt the power of God flow through my hand to her. In less than a half-hour she was fully restored to life.

How we rejoiced and praised God for his tremendous miracle! Everyone heard her tell of it, and later I would tell it to thousands throughout the world. My Mother had suffered a fatal heart attack, we found out, and she had been taken to heaven. Sent back to earth by the Lord, she returned to a fully restored heart and body. She did not experience heart trouble again.

Little did I know that at time, this miracle was an important step in preparing for my escape from Romania. Fifteen years before the escape, a woman of God declared that God was going to deliver me from our communist country to serve the Lord in the outside world; yet I lacked faith to believe such a thing then.

How does the Lord increase faith? I know that for me it was through difficult and grueling experiences. I had to go through hard things with the KGB secret police, arrests, beatings, interrogation, and trial by the government. Through suffering and learning how to trust God I was ultimately prepared for God's deliverance from Communist Romania.

It is amazing what God will do once we turn our lives wholly over to Him. As it says in Hebrews 11:32-34:

And what shall we say? For the time would fail me to tell of Gideon, and of Barak, and of Samson, and Jephthae, of David also, and Samuel, and of the prophets; who through faith subdued kingdoms, wrought righteousness, obtained promises, stopped the mouths of lions, quenched the violence of fire, escaped the edge of the sword, out of weakness were made strong, waxed valiant in fight, turned to flight the armies of the aliens."

Gideon was, in his own view, a nobody and the runt of his tribe and family. Yet through yielding to Almighty God, equally obscure and ordinary individuals have become great men and women of faith. God did mighty things, delivering an entire nation because of Gideon's simple, lamb-like faith and trust. Gideon's God will do the same for us today!

I will never forget the case of a couple in Romania who trusted the Lord in the face of an impossible situation. I went to visit close Christian friends in their home one day. The man was an engineer, and his wife, Pania, a medical doctor. According to the custom in Christian households, the first thing we did when I arrived was pray. As we prayed I received a vision of Pania holding a white lamb in her hands. I described the vision to Pania and her husband. Afterwards, they wondered what it meant. I told them that God intended to give them a child.

"Everything is possible with God," was all that I could tell her at the time. Almost a year passed. One day I again visited the couple. After our first prayer time I was embarrassed to tell Pania what I had just seen in a vision: a lovely, white lamb lying on her bed.

Her face lit up with a radiant smile. "You know, God has given us a beautiful little girl," she said. Pania left the room quickly, then returned in a moment with a little baby girl.

Today this "little lamb" is a medical doctor in the United States.

Chapter 5: "A Second Heaven"

With a growing ministry in the underground churches (Elijah began preaching and doing evangelistic work in 1958; Bible smuggling in 1959), I had to go great distances to visit believers all over the country. But I could not travel such great distances on foot. Even on a bicycle it would be nearly impossible. I needed motorized transportation.

After two years training and graduation from maintenance mechanics school (1960), I continued work as a maintenance mechanic at the clothing factory. In about 1970, I changed my trade to that of a plasterer (no frescoes in those days!) employed in government projects. But despite long hours, the pay was so low I would never be able to buy anything beyond a bicycle.

But God blessed me financially. I was eventually able to purchase a motorcycle for use in ministry. The motorcycle was of tremendous use. Yet later, for extending ministry to the Russian-occupied portions of Romania across the border, I would have need of two more wheels.

Cars are an even greater impossibility to a blue-collar workman than motorcycles! In Romania there were trains for cross-country travel, some public transportation for city commuters, and bicycles for the masses. Government officials and the KGB secret police (who operated fleets of sleek, powerful Volgas serviced in secret garages) drove cars.

God saw an even greater need, however, than transportation. I had come to think of myself as a worker in God's kingdom in the same way I was a worker in government construction. He sent an angel to our house one day in 1963. "Come one second with me to heaven," the angel said.

It was a complete surprise. Taken by the angel, my spirit was lifted instantly into heaven. Hallelujah! Praise God! I found myself in heaven's city, walking the grand streets and gazing awestruck at all the throngs of people and buildings. I saw Abraham, Isaac, Jacob and prophets such as Moses and Samuel, all very much alive and vigorous. I do not know how they appeared on earth, but in heaven they were tall and about thirty-three years of age. I watched the saints approach and there was no need to speak, for with them I could communicate perfectly without saying a word! When the heavenly second was over, the angelic guide returned me to the bedroom where I sat weeping.

My eyes had beheld such glory I could not bear the thought of earth! At the thought of having to take part again in this drab and difficult life, I could not stop the tears. Finally, God put a stop to my sorrowing. He revealed why He had brought me to heaven for that "second":

"Stand fast therefore in the liberty wherewith Christ hath made us free, and be not entangled again with the yoke of bondage." Galatians 5:1

Though I had started out right, I had somehow been overtaken by chains and thrown into a quarry of my own making:

> *Beneath a peak Arabian,*
> *Gaped a pit deep dug by man,*
> *Each slave that labored there 'til dark—*
> *Branded, doomed with Hagar's mark.*

In Romanian society, communism has reduced wages to the point where a man works strenuously all day for enough to buy a mere chicken. But the best workers who continue to labor under such a system are rewarded—draped from chin to belt with ribbons and medals and treated to a banquet they will not see again until they have somehow surpassed another quota at the factory.

The Apostle Paul fought against this creeping in of Hagar's mark and the terrible yoke of self-righteousness in the early church.

True children of the God of grace
Often end in fleshly works;
Faithful once, they lose the race,
Ensnared by nets a fowler jerks.
"From Jerusalem to Corinth and Rome he preached:"
"There is therefore now no condemnation to them which are in Christ Jesus. For the law of the Spirit of life in Christ Jesus hath made me free from the law of sin and death!" (Romans 8: 1-2)

It took a trip all the way to heaven to show what I had foolishly laid aside—the fathomless, wondrous grace of Jesus Christ our Righteousness. The clock told me that the "second" in heaven had lasted three hours on earth. How different is God's time! I also know from this "one second" trip in 1963 how utterly different from man's works is the grace of God.

It is true that communism's hold was forced on people, but there are legalistic bondages that afflict believers just as cruelly. Even as brave Romanian people all through history fought against tyranny and sacrificed their blood and lives for Christ and freedom, believers in Jesus need to resist Hagar's mark.

And so I ask, are we freeborn?
Cephas-like, we're shysters still?
O Lord, we come to thee forlorn,
Our bonds are strong, our spirits ill.
"Jesus was once again the Savior over-flowing with amazing grace:"
I am Christ-born, His blood freed me.
How can I then to chains return?
For one red drop of liberty
My godly deeds I gladly burn.

It was a lesson of paramount importance that I did not learn completely in 1963. Years later, my wife and I were having trouble with our teenage son. We prayed night and day for him, yet his waywardness increased.

The Lord showed me, however, that I was the problem: my self-righteous way of treating him was only making things worse. "But what was I to do?" I asked the Lord in great desperation.

"Just love him," Jesus said.

And the Lord was right. Against HIS love there is no law, nor, in this case, could there be much resistance. Our son returned home, responding to Christ's love and grace. Today he loves and serves the Lord with all his heart.

Chapter 6: "The Iron Collar"

"*...Joseph, who was sold for a servant [slave], whose feet they hurt with fetters; he was laid in iron until the time that his word came [to pass]: the word of the Lord tried him.*" (Psalm 105: 17-19)

Joseph was seventeen, a shepherd lad, when he was torn from his family and sold as a fettered slave to Egypt. Many years passed before the former slave was appointed Prime Minister of Egypt and was re-united with his father, Jacob. Yet as a boy back in Canaan, Joseph had dreamed that one day he would be raised up above his family, so that they would all bow to him. Some translations speak of his feet being bound with fetters and an iron collar round his neck, though the original Hebrew indicates his entire body was "laid in iron." However his condition is described, the scriptures clearly speak of testing. For Joseph the glorious fulfilment of his dreams entailed a long and faithful wait on God amidst trying circumstances.

Have you too been waiting a long time on God for something very important? For your health, your provision, for a mate, for deliverance from bad circumstances? For a turn-around in your marriage? For the salvation of your loved ones or family or children? Whatever it is, you can look at Joseph and his example will show what it takes to endure and finally obtain the answers to God's glorious promises. For me it was a long wait too, joined by my wonderful wife, with whom I continued to wait, trusting God for the eventual fulfilment of His promises. This is the "Joseph experience" of every true child of God. Do not run from it. Let God take you through. However difficult and long, the process will make you what God wants, not break you as it may seem to be doing just now. Let God take you through. He will not ever fail you!

People in the Western countries are often unaware of how long people have been wearing iron collars in Romania, waiting for release amidst crushed and shattered dreams. But instead of looking to God for deliverance, as Joseph did, millions cross their wrists as a symbol of their bondage and despair...and their fetters screw even tighter.

As a Soviet Union ally, Romania was required to supply slave labor to Soviet projects such as the Danube-to-Adriatic canal. The barge canal was a scheme for bypassing the Turkish-controlled Bosporus and more effectively draining the Romanian "bread-basket" of its foodstuffs. Tens of thousands of Romanians (and others) were imprisoned and assigned to slave gangs to dig communist East Europe's own version of the Suez Canal. Engineers were shot who said that the project was impractical. The insane work was abandoned, but not before multitudes had perished from squalor, disease, and maltreatment.

The God of Joseph, indeed, was merciful. He spared my life while such atrocities were going on. I never had to take part in the Danube canal fiasco. But over twenty years would pass before God's promise to set me free would be fulfilled, and I had to experience the attacks of the KGB, arrest, and interrogation, and all sorts of harassment.

After I was finally set free in 1974 and was visiting West Germany, I was befriended by a fine Christian family and met a modern "Joseph" who had been waiting for God's fulfilment of a dream. While praying with them, God gave me a word for him: "I will use you, my son, and you will be a blessing to many people, for I will do a miracle for you."

Johannes was a successful banker and looked nothing like Joseph the Hebrew slave in Egypt. Inside the tailored suit and immaculate shirt was a man of God who had a heart to serve the Lord full-time in a special ministry. Like Joseph, he had received a promise from God.

He, too, had to wait a long and difficult time for its fulfilment. He had already been waiting about ten years before we met.

In a vision I saw a house God would give Johannes for use in serving the Lord's people. It was large and beautiful, with many windows. It was set in a part of Germany famed for forest scenery. Johannes wrote the vision down and no more was said about it. I left Germany and did not hear from Johannes for years. Then I received a letter from Johannes with a change of address. "Please come and visit us any time in our home," he wrote. When I revisited Germany, Johannes met me at the train station. Greeting each other, we might have noted the passing of seven years in each other's face. But Johannes had something else on his mind, for he asked if I remembered the vision about the house. "Do you think you would know the house if you saw it?" he questioned me.

Since I could still see it in my mind's eye I said, "Yes," and off we went in his car After a kilometer or two he pulled over to the roadside and pointed. "Is that the house?" he asked. "No," I replied. Again, we drove, then stopped abruptly. "How about that house over there?" Again: "No." Johannes did this several times, and then he halted by a large building. "That's the house God showed me in a vision seven years ago!" I exclaimed.

Johannes showed me the facility God gave him. The "house" contains a 50-room hotel and a fine restaurant, and is the meeting place of a church as well. It is a unique setting for rest and Christian fellowship in a society ridden with anxiety and fear. It is also proof that years ago Johannes dreamed beautiful things and, most significantly, had the patience to wait on Joseph's glorious God. This is something all of us children of God can do.

Chapter 7: "Isaac And Rebecca"

Elijah, my fiery namesake, was another favorite Bible character to me. I was very impressed by his obedience and awesome miracles. But what about Isaac as a man of God? I confess that I was, initially, less excited about him.

Can anyone number his miracles? Did he ever slay four hundred false prophets? Call down fire from heaven against his enemies? Or outrun the speeding "Volga" of King Ahab? Isaac did nothing particularly spectacular his whole life. He lived, had some rather unruly children, and died. Yet his life was not in vain. His story might not excite us, but he was a most spiritual man. Isaac was the heir of promise. All he needed to do for fulfilment was rest—rest and abide in God amidst his various difficulties.

His home, a camp in a wilderness desert, was the house of God. As a youth Isaac was a boy with a lamb's nature. He let himself be laid on the altar of bloody sacrifice by his own father, without protest or cries for help. As a grown man, he waited serenely on God to provide a wife. He was forty years old (his beloved mother, Sarah, had been dead three years) when God gave him the perfect helpmate, beautiful Rebecca.

But long BEFORE Rebecca came to fill his empty arms, Isaac needed to discover how to rest in God and trust him in every circumstance of life. How did Isaac do it? Isaac could not read about God (and divine rest) in the Bible. There was no Bible! He was a shepherd like his father, Abraham. For such there was no Bible college or Nicean Creed or any other guide to the knowledge of God. Isaac had "only" the Spirit of God in the context of the realities of life. He had to

30

discover God without modern "advantages". Yet Isaac succeeded so well that he became renowned for knowing God's rest. A generation of his descendants later perished in the Sinai wilderness because they failed to follow Isaac's example.

In my own future, resting Isaac's way proved a matter of life and death. After marriage, my wife and I lived in Dornesti for a time. We built a house that was designed to hold secret meetings of the underground church. I also kept Bibles there until they could be delivered to Christians in Soviet Russia. From about 1959 through 1974 the year of my escape, smuggling Bibles and nurturing the underground church in Romania and Russia were my primary functions in the Kingdom of God.

It was dangerous undertaking to supply Bibles to needy Christians in such areas. Our local police, alerted by the KGB, ransacked our home two or three times a month to find the Bibles. These raids could be expected nearly anytime of the day or night, but seldom were they expected in the very late night and early morning hours.

But one morning Aurica and I had just finished laying Bibles in a hole under the floor of a room and were astonished to hear the police at the door. They were early, and we were caught with the Bibles in plain view, covered only with a sheet of plastic to keep off the dust. Moreover, Aurica had laid more Bibles under some of our children's clothing in their room.

Aurica shuddered. Our executions for hiding Bibles were a foregone conclusion. Romanian police were known to torture people to death. All I could do was pray and refuse to give in to panic. The police searched the entire house, room by room, and passed by both caches of Bibles without saying a word, as if the Bibles were not even there! Angrily they stomped out of the house. The moment we were alone we realized what had happened. God had blinded them!

Some years before my marriage, I had gone to visit Sister Maria. Maria was my mother's old friend who had known much persecution but had survived every fiery trial. I knew she could pray and receive a true word of guidance from the Lord. Since I was entertaining the thought of a major trip for ministry to the southeast area of Romania, I went to her for prayer.

This wonderful old saint prayed, and I was delighted when she told me she had a word from God for me. God said through her: "I will bless you on this trip. Step by step, I will guide you. You will see My hand. And I will bless you as I blessed Isaac." She also described what she saw while praying. She said God would set me gloriously free, and like a mighty eagle I would soar over the highest mountains and be a witness of Jesus to many people in foreign countries.

I was overwhelmed. But, even though her vision agreed with the words of the angel given to me as a shepherd boy, I could not then believe I was going to be set free from Romania. Yet, knowing how godly and trustworthy this woman of God was, I put the amazing words away into my heart for safekeeping and reference.

Later, as I traveled to southeast Romania, I had no thought of marriage. My thoughts were more taken up with the fact that I knew virtually no one along the entire route.

As I drove through the lovely, green hills and valleys of the countryside, God gave me the clear direction that Sister Maria had foreseen. I had already gone 300 kilometers when He spoke and told me what to do. Coming to Cluj, a city unknown to me, I was to turn right after the first bridge.

I crossed the bridge and pulled over to the right of the road. Some children rushed up to admire the motorcycle. I gave them some candy and instantly we were friends. "Do you know any Christians?" I asked. A boy pointed across the street. "Christians live there," he said. "But be careful, for they have a big dog. If you aren't a Christian, he will know it, and you are in big trouble."

Laughing a little to myself, I entered the fenced yard. As I entered I saw the big dog running at me. But then he skidded to a halt and his tail started wagging. A voice called out. I turned to see an old, white-haired gentleman beckoning to me from the house. "Welcome, brother!" he said. "My dog did not bark, so I know that you are a Christian. Please come in!"

So, the young lad was telling the truth about the dog! Amazed, I followed the kindly old man into the house and we were soon friends. Zadok, who is about 95 years of age now, still lives in Romania (as of 1989), shepherding God's little flock. He told me that he had been praying for God to send His servant to help him in the church that met in his home He was certain I was God's answer.

Because of these remarkable circumstances, it was obvious to me that God had led me to this house and this secret, underground church. Recognizing God's leading, I stayed with Pastor Zadok. At the meeting that night many people came. God blessed the meeting, giving me His word, poems and visions. These encouraged and strengthened the people. God was able to do such a work in their hearts that a powerful awakening of the people's faith broke out. I did not catch any sleep until late in the morning, when I lay down on the floor because there was no available bed.

Zadok also gave a word to me that was a perfect duplicate of the word from God given to me in Dornesti through Sister Maria.

I left Cluj and continued on another 300 kilometers. I was praying as I approached another large city. "Lord," I said, "I know someone here, but I don't have the address." God promptly answered and told me to go until I saw some sheep; then I was to cross the street and wait by them. Entering the city, I stopped by the first sheep that I saw. There were only a few sheep, a very small flock. I waited for something to happen. Presently, I saw a man coming. "Hello," I said to the shepherd. "May I speak with you?"

He listened as I started speaking about sheep. I asked if he knew the Good Shepherd, Jesus. He gave me a close and friendly look. "He is my Lord," he said. "I am a shepherd, too," I said.

After a few more words, the man led the way to his house. He too pastored a little flock of underground church Christians. Invited to the meeting that night, I was able to minister to the people with poems and visions that the Lord gave just for them. God was obviously blessing this trip with special opportunities for ministry. Before I could leave one of them had a word from God for me. He said "that God would bless me as He had blessed Isaac"!

I returned to the main road to continue my journey. At last, the distinguished profile of the regional capital of Timisoara came into view. It, too, was a large city, but far more Western and cosmopolitan in style than other Romanian cities. Its environs were very photogenic with a rich, productive plain, a forest, and a river.

As God had done all along the way, He directed me to a village on the city's edge, close by the Timis River. My uncle came from the house where the Lord had me stop! He had not seen me since I was a small boy, so he was very happy to see me after all these years. Now I was 24 years old.

I stayed several days with him, preaching short messages to the underground church that met in his home. I shared poems with them as well. At one of the meetings a man approached me with a word from God: "I will help you. I brought you here because I want to bless you like I blessed my servant, Isaac."

Word for word! Yet again God's promise concerning this trip had come to me unmistakably—for I had told no one. But I still felt I was not ready for God's "blessing." I was not looking to be married just yet. I had to tell the Lord how reluctant I felt, but I still wanted to obey Him just the same. The man of God continued the message to me: "Tomorrow morning, I will give you a sign. The sign will be this. The first girl you see tomorrow will ask the question, 'What are you looking for?'"

My uncle overheard the man's words. I was somewhat stunned.

The next morning my uncle asked me to go on a visit to another pastor-friend's home. We found the home, but he was gone. His wife said he was in another village visiting. So we continued walking. My uncle was in front when we came upon a lone girl in the street. She was sweeping the sidewalk in front of her house. I stopped. It was as if a hand had reached out and grabbed my arm, stopping me in my tracks. I stood looking at the girl. "What are you looking for?" she asked demurely, in a childlike, soft voice.

My uncle, hearing the girl's question, turned around and laughed.

"We have been expecting God's servant to come," she added. "And I know you are God's child." I must have stared at her with my mouth open. Simply dressed, with a small scarf on her light-brown hair, she looked at me with shy, yet interested eyes. I wondered what to do.

I soon learned her name was Aurica (pronounced "ow-rick-kah"). She invited me to meet her father, a pastor of a church. I was taken into their home. All the family and people there soon heard the story. I too listened as Aurica told how God had answered her prayer. Long before I appeared, she had been praying and fasting. Someone gave her a word that God had chosen a husband for her, and that he would come to her home seven weeks after she stopped her fast. It was indeed so. I had come on the very day appointed by God.

In spite of all this, I still withheld saying anything about the promises and words from God I had received relating to Isaac and Rebecca. Still waiting on God, I wanted to seek Him and determine that this was truly His will. After I left her home, our paths unexpectedly crossed again, this time in the market place. Of all things, she was buying some things for MY mother. I felt great joy and peace when I saw Aurica.

Returning to Dornesti, I spent the next few months seeking God's will. Meanwhile, Aurica and I corresponded. We both knew that God could bring Christians together in marriage. I had heard of absolute strangers in Soviet Russia being brought together and married because God had chosen them for each other.

Finally, I knew for certain that God wanted this marriage. I wrote telling Aurica. Within less than a year after meeting, we married in Timisoara, in a regular, daytime church service (1964) after alerting only the pastor and our own families and friends. The pastor was preaching a message on Isaac and Rebecca when our wedding party entered the church! On seeing us, the people were filled with joy! Later, we enjoyed a reception in Aurica's home, with an entire village of several hundred friends, family and relatives crammed into the small house.

Chapter 8: "Before the Council"

"*And when they had brought them, they set them before the council: And the high priest asked [interrogated] them.*" (Acts 5: 27)

As newlyweds, we honeymooned in Timisoara, staying in the homes of relatives. Taking long strolls, we enjoyed the spring weather. Flowers, butterflies, and birdsong as from the pages of the Song of Solomon beautified Timisoara's many parks.

Our wedding was still much in our thoughts. We could not forget the surprise and joy on the faces of the people when a real bride and bridegroom entered the church—just as the pastor was preaching about Isaac and Rebecca! He told how Abraham had sent his steward to far off Padan-Aram to seek a wife for his son Isaac. Guided by the Spirit of God, the steward was led straight to Rebecca. There also came a specific word to us: "God will bless this marriage. It is to God's glory."

But soon it came time to turn away from Timisoara and move to Dornesti, far to the north on the Romanian-Soviet border.

Moving from the more urbanized life of the Banat region to the mountain country of Moldavia-Bucovina brought a dramatic change, but Aurica was trusting in her refuge under God's wings. She soon settled into her new nest. Since we lived with my mother until our own house was ready, Aurica had convenient help when our first child arrived (also in 1964). Early in the marriage God told Aurica we would have ten children! Yet she did not falter in the decision she had made, though she had come from a small family of five.

Aurica was a dedicated believer in Jesus from twelve years of age. Her mother and father were devout Christian parents. When she became a wife and mother she was equipped with her own special armor. God had given her a gift of hospitality. She knew how to help others in a gracious way, with deep compassion for the poor. She was given clear dreams that imparted specific direction for us to take in difficult times. Her dreams also enabled her to put away fears and doubts when she was later confronted by thoughts of dangers involved in my escape from Romania.

For three years we stayed with my mother while we built a new house nearby. The house was designed for underground church meetings so there was one large room, while the remaining family rooms were kept small. It was cement and stucco (for I had learned these trades at work), a simple white cottage.

We began the house on faith, for the cost was impossible to afford for a common workman, however long he saved. My government construction wages were so low we had to budget very careful. We could not have survived unless we raised most of our food in our garden, along with chickens, geese, and a few sheep.

It was a miracle of God that we could even begin to build. Yet somehow, we always had means to continue, moving into the unfinished house and working on it until it was completed. The fact this house was not affordable on a workman's salary later brought trouble with the government, which being atheistic refuses to acknowledge God's proven ability to help His children do impossible things. In five years, the new house was finished. But just two years afterwards, God told us to leave and move back to Timisoara in preparation for our deliverance from Romania. We had spent five years building our new house. But as we built the house, God was building our faith. That was his real purpose.

Yet, before we were delivered, more faith-building opportunities came our way. They all had to do with our membership and involvement with the underground church of God, and Bible deliveries into the hands of fellow believers in Soviet lands. With the lives of our children at stake, we were painfully aware of the fact that any wrong step could be fatal. Yet, as evangelical believers determined to follow Christ and the path of the Cross, we knew there was little chance of avoiding trouble with the authorities, however much we wanted peace.

We would not have suffered as much if we had walked the broader path of impersonal and formal religion. Over ninety percent of Romanians have a formal church background, whether or not they hold communist party membership. Maybe once or twice a year they attend services (though there are always more devout individuals). But for those who meet every other night and stress the reality of a personal relationship with Jesus Christ, the path is indeed narrow.

State control over the economy was totally established. Efforts to control all other aspects of national life also received top priority in the communist Romanian state. Religion was made the responsibility of a government bureau and all churches had to be registered in order to be recognized as legitimate religious bodies (just as, in America, all Indian tribes must be registered with the Federal Bureau of Indian Affairs in order to be recognized as legitimate tribes that can claim government aid—Editor).

Registry, of course, entailed government supervision and constant scrutiny to insure that baptisms and evangelism—so vital in evangelical circles—did NOT take place. Most Christians, evangelical and orthodox, complied, because the regime thought nothing of using mass imprisonment and execution.

So it was, in order to be free to follow the Lord completely, that Aurica and I chose to be part of the bitterly persecuted underground church that met secretly. To be caught meant huge fines, unpayable with common wages. When the fines could not be paid there was imprisonment. Caught three times at a secret meeting, a believer was sent to prison. That could entail torture, loss of a job and expulsion of his children from school.

Communist countries are more than happy to show Western tourists and distinguished churchmen lofty constitutions that guarantee freedom of religion. Certain government-registered churches are always shown as examples of how freely Christians can worship in a communist society. Yet Christians who want to be free suffer greatly in such societies. They are condemned to lurking in the forests to escape detection, meeting late at night in private homes, only to suffer huge fines and imprisonment when caught. This is what it costs them to follow Christ as He, and not the atheist government, would lead. Nevertheless, these people pray continually for their persecutors, knowing who is the real foe.

I heard of a little boy who witnessed of his Savior in school. "How can anyone see God?" the teacher scoffed. "No one can see this Jesus of yours!" Yet the boy was not at a loss. The eighth verse from Chapter 5 in the Gospel of Matthew came instantly to his mind, "Blessed are the pure in heart, for they shall see God." The instructor severely chastised him as soon as he spoke these words of Jesus.

At Dornesti came a word from God. He intended to set us free. But it was also God's plan to send me out of Romania first, without Aurica and the children. Later, we were to reunite in some free country.

Having known and suffered relentless persecution as Christians, we wanted to experience freedom of belief. But Aurica did not have peace when she heard I was to go alone and she was to follow with the children by the way God would provide. She grew more disturbed when we heard about a Christian friend who was shot and killed trying to cross the border. It was vital that we be united in heart in this matter. A wife and family cannot be left temporarily behind without mutual agreement and trust.

God made our two minds to agree in this way. Aurica dreamed two dreams. First, she saw a great, rushing river with me swimming across. She could see I was a powerful swimmer, able to overcome the strong current of the river. I reached the far shore safely where angels stood on guard against the soldiers and police dogs that patrolled the river's edge. In the second dream Aurica saw me crossing the river in a boat pulled by angels. Again, I was brought safely to the farther shore and was able to go on my way unmolested because I had been made invisible to the eyes of the soldiers.

Aurica understood that the "river" was the border. She had seen God's mighty deliverance and His almighty power to bring me safely across, surrounding me with protecting angels, despite the guards and dogs.

I will never forget the look on her face when she told me her dreams. Her face was shining with joy and peace. God had given her His rich grace to understand and accept His chosen way.

Meanwhile, I continued to work as a plasterer and minister to a church that met in our little, white house. We also continued to make Bibles available to fellow Christians in Soviet lands.

For years, the supplying of Bibles was a burning concern of our hearts. Romanian Christians had a much greater access to the Bible than Jesus' flock in the Soviet Union. The USSR was more determinedly atheistic than some of its satellites such as Greek Orthodox Romania and Catholic Poland. Lavishing millions of rubles on a center for atheism in Moscow, the KGB gave top priority to stopping the entry of Bibles into the USSR (though officially there was no law against Bibles in the USSR).

As far as the KGB was concerned, Bibles were considered to be as powerful and dangerous as plastic explosives, or bombs. Terror-stricken at the supposed threat to their power, the secret police treated people severely who were caught bringing God's scriptures into the USSR. We also knew Romanian authorities supported Soviet anti-Bible policies. So we realized that a single misstep of ours would likely bring torture and death. We had to depend on God every minute. Otherwise we could not have survived in this extremely dangerous work.

Years passed. As we continued to supply Bibles undetected, we succeeded in bringing another kind of persecution upon us: government trial. Aurica and I were amazed to learn that the government intended to sue us because we lived in a house of our own that they said we could not afford on a workman's salary. Naturally, the case was already decided against us when we first heard of it. Once they decided to bring us to trial, we already stood convicted in the eyes of the law. It only remained for the government judge to declare our punishment. Everyone in Dornesti soon heard of the coming trial. They all said we would lose the house. There would also be enormous fines and lengthy imprisonment, according to them.

The first trial began. The prosecutor reviewed the files of my income for a ten-year period. Then he subtracted how much it cost us to live. On that basis he charged that we could not possibly build a house.

Questioned, I told the court that God had enabled us, bit by bit, to build a house. Furthermore, I told the court that He is a God who can do the impossible. I also said that the house they assessed at 200,000 lei had actually cost me only about 50,000 lei (about $12,00 US) because my relatives helped me to do the work. My only expense was the materials.

Yet the government intended to fine me 150,000 lei! They reasoned that I had somehow obtained the money illegally, and now I must pay for my "crime."

Since nothing but these unsupported charges surfaced at the trial, the judge was very upset because he could not declare us guilty. Everyone was amazed when we were let go. But our rejoicing did not last long. A higher court, hearing the decision, ruled that the lower court had made a mistake, justifying a retrial.

Facing a second, grueling year, we sought God again for His deliverance. He answered by providing an excellent lawyer with a lion's fearless heart. He stood up against the government's charges, reviewing my entire life in detail using government records. He than charged the government with harassment of an honest, hard-working citizen! The lawyer proved me to be a thrifty working man who had succeeded in building a house for his family...even buying a car. By the time he finished speaking, he had shown conclusively that not a thread of the government's evidence could stand against my public record. The judge and prosecutor were struck speechless. Then the judge ruled that the charges be thrown out. We had won—against the seemingly almighty government! Such a thing was truly impossible and is still being talked about in Romania today.

We had seen God's truly almighty power deliver us from our foes. Our faith was greatly strengthened, and we felt we could not believe God for our escape from Romania. Nobody had ever beaten the government in court. No wonder people told us we could not win and that our situation was hopeless. "Jesus is the Way," I replied. "We are not finished, for Jesus gives victory." We kept hearing that everything would be taken away from us, that we would lose our home. "No way," I told them. "It belongs to God." Then later, when they heard about the victory they said to me, "You must have ten Jewish heads in one." But they were mistaken. I am not the brilliant man of jurisprudence and law that they thought—I was just a plasterer on government projects. "It's not me, it is God," I said.

Aurica and I truly knew what Peter was talking about when he wrote to encourage others concerning various trials of faith.

"Wherein ye greatly rejoice, though now for a season, if need be, ye are in heaviness through manifold temptations, that the trial of your faith, being much more precious than of gold that perisheth, though it be tried with fire, might be found unto praise and honor and glory at the appearing of Jesus Christ." (I Peter 1: 6-7)

Chapter 9: "Can You Help Us?"

During the two-year period of the government trials, our home was repeatedly searched for incriminating evidence. This search is called, in Romania, an "inventory". The inventory takes the form of a surprise raid, with confiscation of any valuable property. Before one of these inventories we were alerted in advance by a close friend, the mayor of Dornesti. He had been my childhood friend. I taught him to ride the motorcycle. As grown men we remained close friends. After the trials he became a Christian and later would suffer imprisonment for his faithfulness to Christ.

The police arrived for the inventory and burst into our home unannounced. As part of the raid they were supposed to "seal" or impound our car. We would never see it again, of course. Everyone, up until the final decision of the second, higher court, never expected us to win the case. God intervened, however. Hallelujah! He had shown repeatedly how He could blind the enemy's eyes. It was a simple matter for Him to erase memories as well. They left after the search, totally forgetting to seal the car that stood by the house! It was a very important failure on their part, for it meant I could still use the car.

God then told me to drive the car to Timisoara and sell it, deposit the money in a secret place, and return home. That meant a long and dangerous trip. Would I even get to Timisoara? Of course I would! God had spoken, and He would watch over my going and coming!

I had no sooner set out than the police, realizing their gross oversight, returned to the house in a big hurry to seal the car. They were very upset when they saw that the car was gone, and questioned

Aurica about my whereabouts. She told them to ask my supervisor at work. Contacted, he then told them to go check at the factory's headquarters, located 300 kilometers away. "Maybe he's been called there," he said. Thus, the police were diverted, while I headed in the opposite direction!

As the old Moskovitz chugged faithfully up and around the Alps of Transylvania, the highest peaks of Romania (which had been a sanctuary for the Romanian people against oppressors countless of times in history), I prayed and sought my "hiding place"—Almighty God.

I had no written permission from the authorities to be on the road. I cried unto the Lord in my predicament. If the police stopped me, driving a car they wanted to impound, they would surely identify me also as the man currently under trial by the government.

Imagine my surprise when I noticed occupants in the car! They were angels! I don't know how I was able to keep driving as the angels spoke of how the Enemy was going to try to frighten me. But they declared that God would guide and protect me against anything men tried to do. The moment the angels disappeared I found myself unable to drive. I pulled over, rejoicing and shaking in equal amounts. I controlled my tears of joy and then proceeded down the road. Ahead I saw hitchhikers. I would have gone by if I had not felt a distinct nudge...since I never stopped unless directed.

The young couple got in. Thankfully, they were Christians, not KGB agents posing as ordinary hitchhikers. They could not help noticing me rejoicing in the Lord, so they identified themselves as one in the same faith. I shared with them the joy the angels' appearance had given and soon after, I let them off at their destination. They were newlyweds. They were grateful for the unexpected fellowship.

Eventually, I reached the large city of Brasov. A few miles outside the city I saw police ahead on the road, motioning for me to pull over. This was the worst thing that could happen, but I remembered the Lord's promise. Instead of asking for my travel permit (a regular procedure on Romanian roads), they had a strange request. "Can you help us" the chief sergeant inquired after a glance at my license plate. "We have a dangerous, violent criminal at the village station near here. We can do nothing with him. When we try to restrain him, he is so powerful he cannot be held long enough to be handcuffed. We will have to shoot him if you cannot help us subdue him."

The chief sergeant further explained that they wanted to transport the man to the main headquarters in Brasov. They wanted me, a stranger to the area, to speak to him, and say anything that might possibly get him to go with me in my car, while a police car followed us to the headquarters. On the dashboard of my car was a picture of Jesus as the Good Shepherd. The officer saw it. "You a Christian? Maybe it would be good for you to tell him about Christian things," he said. "And don't be afraid. I will be sitting right behind you, if he gives any trouble I will shoot him.

Having been forewarned and assured by God, I agree to help the police and was conducted to a nearby village police station. The man was exactly what they described. Massively built, unafraid of any man or authority, he looked as if he had broken all the laws of man and God. The police told the man that they had brought someone to speak to him, a visitor from another part of the country who would be taking him to a meeting in Brasov. Thus, introduced in a friendly way, we walked to my car, and the man got in.

As we drove toward Brasov I began to speak to the man about the love of Jesus. I could see his expression soften as he looked at the picture of Jesus on the dashboard.

It took about an hour for us to reach the police headquarters. Brasov was so large and unknown to me that I had to be directed street by street until we finally came to our destination. By that time, the man's face was very changed. By his expression I could see that his guilty, sin-hardened heart had been profoundly touched.

Police immediately surrounded our car (for it was no "meeting" but an arrest). The man got out and was put in restraints, but he did not resist. "Here I am in your hands," he said to the amazed police. Submitting meekly to arrest, he was led away. The police then turned to me in gratitude. "Fill your car with gas, Comrade!" they said. So, my car was filled with gas at the KGB pump in main headquarters, while in another part of the country the police were furiously searching all the roads for a certain Moskovitz and its driver!

Free to go, I drove to Timisoara without incident, and stayed the night with Christian friends. In the morning I placed an ad in the newspaper. The paper appeared the next day and I received an instant response. I sold the car and entrusted the money to a Christian friend.

Returning to Dornesti, I was immediately confronted by the police. "We'll arrest you for this!" they stormed. "We may even kill you. Where is the car?" "I had to sell the car, so we might have enough money to live," I said. "Where is the money?" they demanded, shaking clenched fists. "That is not your business," I said. "Why do you ask for my money? You took me to court. The court has yet to make a decision. You still have to wait. The car is sold." "But we were supposed to seal the car the same time we took inventory," they protested pathetically. "I am sorry, that is your mistake," I said.

Later, news came to us that one poor policemen was made a scapegoat for the others. Held responsible for the loss of the car, he was uprooted from his home and stationed clear across the country.

Chapter 10: "Under Arrest"

"*Now about that time Herod the king stretched forth his hand to vex [imprison and execute] certain of the church. And he killed James the brother of John with the sword. And because he saw it pleased the Jews [the high priests and Pharisees], he proceeded to take Peter also.*" (Acts 12: 1-3a)

I had to endure numerous arrests by the government, police and the KGB. An arrest could last two or three days, or weeks. But until they had enough evidence to convict, they could legally keep me only so long without a sentence of imprisonment. So, each time I was arrested I was eventually sent home after the usual tactics were inflicted. Whenever I was beaten, I was told they would kill me if I told anyone.

One time I came home from a police interrogation and my shoulders were twitching uncontrollably from the clubbing. My children asked what had happened to me. But how could I tell them? I suffered much from the spasms, which continued for several days. We prayed for God to stop them, which He did, showing us He not only had control of the arresting authorities but of my muscles as well.

Aurica, two of the children, and I, took a summer vacation. During the three weeks we traveled in the countryside God told me trouble was coming, but I was to be strong and not fear any evil. He promised to put His words in my mouth, and the police would not be able to harm me.

Also, on the trip, I had both a dream and a vision of a man with whom I had indirectly worked in supplying Bibles to Christians in communist lands. He was a few years younger than I, and he was very intelligent and capable. I eventually learned that he had given Bibles to some Russian relatives who were later arrested with the Bibles. The police raided his house, in turn, and they found an additional 3,000 Bibles in his garden. Having seen him in the vision and a dream, though not knowing any of these things, I was concerned and prayed for him.

When we returned home my mother told us that the KGB had been coming every hour of the day and night looking for me. She said the police had been searching the entire country for us. She had no sooner spoken than the police walked into the house and grabbed me. "Now you are in trouble!" they told me. "We have all the facts that we need to convict you." They dragged me in to the main police station, which was becoming a very familiar place.

At last they thought they had a complete case, strong enough to convict me and bring my execution. My "crime" was, of course, Bible smuggling. But despite their ingeniously laid traps, all their plans went awry at the start.

The huge number of people they call in as "witnesses" against me were told to testify that I had given them Bibles. "That's not true," they stoutly declared, despite the threats they had to endure. "This man did not give us any Bibles, we do not know him."

In turn, when I was questioned with each person brought in, there was an unshakable firmness in my stand, imparted by the strengthening of the Holy Spirit. Their testimony, without exception, supported everything I said. If I had at any time spoken one word on my own, or changed my testimony, they would have caught it, with fatal consequences.

Just the same, the police assumed I could not possibly escape this time. They had a prime witness, my friend John, who had been arrested after the thousands of Bibles were unearthed in his garden, and who dazedly claimed, under torture, to be my accomplice in a Bible smuggling ring I supposedly headed.

As the police began interrogating me, John's name began cropping up in the questions. Since God had warned me, I was now alerted to the possible motive behind the arrest. I gradually perceived from their conversation that he had broken down under the relentless interrogation and torture, and that he had "confessed" things I had done which, in fact, I had not done.

They were so sure they had all the facts I was presented with the thick report. They even accused me of starting a conflict between Russia and Romania! "It is not true," I told them. "I have not done anything wrong. I am not a criminal or spy as you say." "Here is the evidence of your crimes," they shouted in my face, showing me the massive document. "We have everything necessary here to convict you. Do you want twenty-five years in prison or execution? It's your choice."

"No, it is not my choice," I replied. "God is over you in this matter, and you cannot do anything on your own. You will do exactly what He tells you to do." This truth infuriated them, and they beat me all the more. Yet God showed He was with me by making my muscles stronger so I could endure the beatings, no matter how long and cruel. "We know everything about you," they blustered. I had to reply, "But if you know everything, why do you ask me so many questions?"

God always gave me the right answers. They could never trip me up in my testimony, though I did not know at times what was coming out of my mouth, due to the lack of sleep.

Finally, they decided to confront me with their major "proof" against me, my friend John. His testimony (I learned later) had broken down at various points, because he could not remember what he had said the previous day. So, he often contradicted himself. They were furious with him for changing his story. "Oh yes, I forgot I said that," he would tell them, but soon would change his story once again under extreme beatings, so that the police were made even more enraged.

"We're going to leave you two alone here" they said to us. "You'll both have to discuss what you did in the past, such as how many thousands of Bibles you, Elijah, sent into Russia through John. Discuss everything about your criminal activities together, and when we come again you will have to tell us the truth." They believed that by putting us together, one would trip the other up, and thus they might get two "birds in one swoop."

Now John had already "confessed" that I had supplied him with thousands of Bibles. The police simply wanted me to convict myself with some slight reaction or assent to John's charges. They reasoned that I would be forced to say something sooner or later in response to him. John and I were put together in a room with two chairs and a small table. We had been told what chairs to take, on either side of the table. He was pale and shaking from the shattering experience of torture and the continual interrogation. I knew exactly what the police intended by bringing us together, but John could not help himself. I knew that he was going to say some unwise things, and that the police would be listening to every word through a tiny electronic "bug" planted on the underside of the table. Of course, John was reduced to a wretched pawn in the merciless hands of the police.

Left alone, we simply looked at one another for a few, suspenseful moments. "Brother Elijah," John began. But I found myself springing to my feet and interrupting him. "What?" I cried, astonished by my own behavior. "You are my brother? You are sure you know me, and you are my brother?" John stared at me and then broke suddenly into laughter. He continued to laugh and could not stop. He was so convulsed with uncontrollable laughter he fell to the floor, holding his sides. A chief officer rushed into the room. "What's going on here?" he demanded to know. but John continued laughing. "I cannot stop!" gasped John. "No brake, no oil!"—a Romanian expression for his absolutely helpless fit. "I cannot stop!" he somehow managed to squeak between terrific peals of laughter. "No brake, no oil..."

I did not say one word to John that could have caused his attack. I simply asked him if he was my brother. But he could not stop laughing.

His attacks were no mere chortles or chuckles. "Just look at the poor fellow!" I cried to the flustered officer. "Take him to the doctor at once and get help immediately!"

John was seized and taken out, still laughing so madly he appeared to be dying of the effects. I did not see him again for hours, but when he was brought back into the room and his eyes fell on me, he exploded once again. Poor John! He was defenseless. Every single time they brought him again to talk with me, the same thing happened. Gales, hurricanes, tornados of hilarity swept dear John away. This went on every day for two weeks! Though I never so much as smiled at John, he was stricken with laughter at the very sight of me. Finally, they stopped bringing John, for the mere sight of the back of my head was enough to give him hysterics.

"Take this man away, please!" I protested each time to the police. "Check him out! Get him some help from the doctor!" They had counted on this face-to-face confrontation to get us to divulge something incriminating, but such a method utterly failed to obtain the necessary evidence for my conviction. John was taken to the prison psychologist who declared he was incurably deranged. The rage and frustration of the police then became so great they would have killed us both on the spot if they had possessed only one atom of legal proof. Forced to let us go free, the police could only gnash their teeth as they thrust us out the prison doors.

A couple of months later I happened to approach John on the street. He was about a block away when he saw me. That was all it took for him to begin laughing uncontrollably as before. After his "medical discharge," he served the Lord without interference for a time, before he was again arrested for Bible smuggling. He was executed in 1983, thirteen years after our mutual incarceration in 1971. This brave man of God had enjoyed a productive extension of his life, and died a martyr.

About a year after the arrest and laughing incident, in April of 1972 I set out to visit God's people across the Romanian-USSR border. I had good reason to go to Chernovitz, the former Romanian capital of the region taken over by the Russian army in World War II. I had many relatives and friends, fellow Christians, in beautiful, old "Cherno," as we called the beloved city.

Only ordinary identification papers were required to cross the northern USSR-Romanian border because both sides were Romanian in population. I checked in at a hotel, and then left after telling the manager I was going to visit friends.

Worshipping God in a meeting of an underground church, I was surprised when the KGB suddenly thrust themselves into the house. As the secret police tore the premises apart in search of Bibles, and searched men, women, and even children, we all continued to pray and seek God for His help. A box of Bibles stood in plain view by the entrance door. If they saw it, we would all be in big trouble, and no doubt I would be held responsible and executed.

The raid was finally concluded. It took some time because there were over one hundred people present. Expert sleuths, the police somehow failed to see the large box by the door. They grabbed me anyway, knowing who I was, the suspect "Bible smuggler." I was taken to prison for interrogation, but they also grilled the manager of the hotel. He was no help to them. He had let me go without inquiring exactly where I was going. Unable to convict me on the basis of the hotel manager's testimony, I was, nevertheless, held three weeks and questioned intensely. Sleep-withholding tactics and beatings of course, accompanied this process.

The Holy Spirit, as He had in the past, gave me every word. Not once did my testimony lapse in consistency as I maintained my innocence against their charges of wrong-doing. The same God who utterly blinded the KGB to the big box of Bibles now frustrated their very attempt to catch me saying something contradictory.

The prime consideration of a jailed man is his date of release. The first day they threw me in a cell I took the opportunity to pray and seek

God to know the date of my release. God answered, giving me a specific date on which I was later, indeed, set free.

God chose to deprive the police of any condemning confession forced from my own lips. Set free, I was sent back to Romania by train. I was re-arrested by Romanian police at the border. My countrymen knew all the details of the Soviet arrest but they tried their old tactics on me for several days. Also failing to convict me of their charges, they too had to set me free. I took the train home and walked to the little white house where no one knew that I had been released. They were still praying and seeking God for my life. The police told my wife that I had killed a man and that I would be in jail forever. The village did not believe it, though some thought I had perhaps accidentally run over someone with the car. Furthermore, Aurica was told that I had committed numerous crimes, a tactic used by police and KGB to smear reputations of Christians and wreck the faith of family members.

I knocked for some time before anyone dared to answer the door. My wife and everyone praying with her could not contain their joy and astonishment. They had not expected to see me alive again.

"And as Peter knocked at the door of the gate, a damsel came to hearken, named Rhoda. And when she knew Peter's voice, she opened not the gate for gladness, but ran in, and told how Peter stood before the gate. And they said unto her, 'Thou art mad.' But Peter continued knocking; and when they had opened the door, and saw him, they were astonished." (Acts 12: 13-17)

In yet another skirmish with the police, I was taken to prison for interrogation. It was the usual round-the-clock ordeal, with the "softening up" of beatings applied to render me pliable enough for making a self-incriminating, verbal blunder. I will never forget the time I was being dragged down a corridor by the guards when they suddenly halted in astonishment. An angel in a general's uniform stood blocking the way, his arm outstretched, pointing to me and ordering that I be released immediately! Without hesitation, the guards obeyed what they thought was a general to all appearances, and I was released!

Chapter 11: "The Burning Lamp"

When the sun sets and it grows dark, people turn on lights. So does God, with His promises and His Word. Though Egypt appeared a very dark place to Moses' parents and his little sister, God had planned the greatest deliverance in history with the Hebrew infant, which he had already announced to Abraham four hundred years before Moses' birth.

A similar promise of deliverance had come to Aurica and me. But a question arose. Were we crazy to believe that we would be set free from Communist Romania? Many had tried to escape and perished in the attempt.

I went to pray with some fellow Christians who knew nothing about God's promise to us. This particular group had never seen me before. Yet at the meeting I received the word from God: "Yes, you have to go, and I will send angels before you and after you, and they will protect you, and I will direct and guide you."

Yet another question arose. Why the Romanian-Yugoslavian border (which God had recently revealed to us)? Though sharing a long border and partners in the communist system, Romania and Yugoslavia were sharply divided and suspicious neighbors at that time. Escapees from Romania received a frigid welcome in Yugoslavia: imprisonment and deportation to Romania. So why would God send us to certain doom? We were already captives in our own country. Why bring more suffering upon ourselves?

Yet God assured us, so much so, that we felt compelled to move to Timisoara near the Yugoslavian border. When my family, friends, and fellow believers heard of our decision, most were put off. Some could understand God's leading in our lives, but many did not want us to move away.

We sold the little white house where so much family and church life had taken place. Furniture and belongings were given away. The authorities allowed us to move, since Aurica had parents and family in Timisoara (in Romania there had to be a good reason for moving, or we would not have been allowed to leave Dornesti).

Aurica carried the baby, Veronica, in her arms as we boarded the train for the day-long trip to Timisoara. It was with bittersweet tears that we took leave of Dornesti, but with joy we reached our destination and fell into the arms of waiting relatives and friends.

At the government labor office, however, I was given another kind of reception. When I applied for work I was told to take a certain construction job. It was the only one available, they claimed. Reluctantly, I had to accept the assignment, though it took me away from my family for long periods—something I knew the authorities wanted. I had to work on government projects in distant cities, returning home sometimes only twice a month. The work of laying cement, plastering, and applying stucco, was hard even for young man, but the greatest hardship was the prolonged separation from family and the church in our home.

The grind of exhausting work, the separation from family and church, and the low pay and lack of advancement proved discouraging. I found a Christian as a work-partner, but I felt a growing sense that I was a stranger living in a hostile, godless society where there was no real chance to live a decent life. As I prayed for Aurica and the children, I also prayed for love, that I might love hard task-masters blinded by communism. They may have hated and despised Christians like me, but the Nail-Pierced One, Jesus, could love the communists who had pierced him, too.

God heard my desperate prayers for strength and love for our enemies, promising that I would be like Jonah. Though I would be taken away from my family for a time, God would protect and deliver me.

After two years, we prayed and fasted all the more for God's deliverance. On my own, I sought every possible way to escape from the country. I contacted people in foreign countries. It all came to nothing. I tried to get work nearer the border, but I was always sent in the opposite direction. I turned to my old supervisor at the factory in Dornesti. He said that he would try to put me on a work project in West Germany; but later he said he could not do it. Finally, God told me to stop "striving," that is, to quit trying to work out my own deliverance. It was not His way.

We had moved in July 1972; it was now 1974. Then, like lightning, a word came from God: "Six months from this day, I will set you free." He also said that two men would appear on the date of release and go with me to freedom. I rushed to the calendar. The date of deliverance was Wednesday, October 9th. It was a glorious word, giving us much needed light and encouragement in a very dark time of our lives.

Again, Aurica and I prayed and fasted and sought God about the escape. I tried to find feasible ways to leave the country, but God again told me to stop and wait only on Him. During the difficult time of waiting, Aurica's faith faced a harder challenge than mine did. It would be easier for me to leave Romania than for her to remain waiting with the family. How would she provide for the family with me out of the country? How long would we be separated? What if I were killed or captured like so many other Christians who had tried to cross the border? What about the KGB when they would come to investigate my disappearance?

Yet God had given her His "burning lamp," the bright assurance of two dreams that promised God's absolute protection for me throughout the border crossing. Even after the dreams, the sacrifice she had to make in her own heart—to entrust me to God along with her children's welfare—was great, and born of much inner struggle and pain. Finally, when her faith had come through, she gained a wonderful peace about letting me go. Only then was our "faith-child" born just like Moses, long before, had been born, to face the test of a voyage in a "basket" of utter dependence upon God woven of struggles and covered with the "pitch" of our own tears.

The last six months of waiting on God were indeed difficult, but they were filled again and again with the light of God's burning lamp of His promises, which grew all the brighter as the day we had marked drew nearer. As with Miriam, the sister of Moses, a glorious deliverance was soon to dawn. We too would one day look in triumph on our foes. Our foes plotted our destruction, but they would be drowned in the sea of confusion and dismay when we escaped from their clutches!

"For Pharaoh went in with his chariots and with his horsemen into the sea, and the Lord brought again the waters of the sea upon them; but the children of Israel went on dry land in the midst of the sea. And Miriam, the prophetess the sister of Aaron, took a timbrel in her hand, and all the women went out after her with timbrels and dances. And Miriam answered them, 'Sing ye to the Lord, for he hath triumphed gloriously; the horse and his rider hath he thrown into the sea.'" (Exodus 15: 19-21)

A taste of the glory of that deliverance at the Red Sea was given to us even before the escape from Romania. Over thirty believers in Christ, mostly young people, gathered in our home for an underground church meeting. We were praying when I found myself declaring, "God is going to do a great miracle for us tonight!" Immediately, I was overcome by dismay. "O Lord!" I cried silently to Him. "Now I am in big trouble. They will all expect a great miracle now." God's response? "Those were My words, not yours," He said.

We went down to the nearby river to conduct baptisms. It was late at night and very dark, the best time for such illegal church work if we wanted to stay out of prison. The waters were dark and cold as we waded into the rushing water. The moment we lifted our hands to God in prayer, a light broke forth, brighter than the midday sun, shining just above our heads. It was no one person's solitary vision. Everyone could see it. The blazing circle of light poured forth singing voices, then lifted slowly and ascended, disappearing into the heavens...only to return at another time as the Light of Deliverance.

Chapter 12: "The Light of Deliverance"

After receiving the six months notice from God, life flowed on much as usual for us in Timisoara. We continued to work, pray and fast, and of course the children needed to be fed, disciplined, schooled, and given godly training. Garden weeds still had to be dug out, the garden watered, and eggs gathered. The domestic animals we kept also required routine attention. The duties and calling of our underground church work and Bible distribution also could not be neglected. So, in all outward aspects our life continued the same as usual, just as it had done for years—yet within our hearts danced a growing excitement we could hardly keep to ourselves. Deliverance, sweet Deliverance, was coming! "La la la la!" our hearts sang within. Deliverance was just around the corner!

Whenever Aurica and I momentarily slipped down off the glistening peak of anticipation at the thought of separation, the Lord gave us a comforting word: "In a short time you will be together again with your family." It gave me much joy to think that God was soon going to fulfill His golden promise to us. In a way, I had waited thirty-three years for this great miracle. Now on the very day it was to become reality, I could not restrain my joy.

It was the same kind of joy that I experienced on the train one time after God revealed that two passengers near me were KGB secret agents. I felt God wanted me to witness to them! But, of course, that was impossible. I knew that the moment I mentioned the slightest thing about Jesus my Savior they would arrest me. Praying and seeking God about this, He gave me such great joy in my spirit that one of the agents, who must have sensed it, turned to me. "How can you be so happy? Why are you so joyful? Tell us!"

Naturally I had to obey their command! So, I told them that the reason for my joy was Jesus, My Lord and Savior. I told them Jesus loved them and wanted to give them joy too. I could see the shock on their faces when they realized what had just happened. They had been given an open testimony of Jesus, but everyone knew they could do nothing to me. I had only followed their orders.

Wednesday, October 9th, 1974 dawned. Aurica and I felt in our spirits that it was the great Day of Deliverance, a glory-filled day made in heaven. So, we were rejoicing every moment, with high expectation we would see God do great and marvelous things.

I arose as usual at 5:00 a.m. to spend time with the Lord, as I always did. I was praying when the promise of Psalm 91 flashed through my mind.

"Because he hath set his love upon Me, therefore I will deliver him; I will set him on high, because he hath known My name. He shall call upon Me, and I will answer him; I will be with him in trouble; I will deliver him, and honor him. With long life will I satisfy him, and shew him My salvation."

Putting my Bible down, I could have wept, for my joy was almost too great to humanly bear. I knew that this was the day the Lord had made, the day Almighty God was going to pull us out of Pharaoh's prison-house and restore our life as down-trodden Christians to freedom, dignity and abundance. I was also expecting to see the two men God had promised would accompany me. They could come at any moment. But I was ready. God had seen to every detail in building our faith, and had even told me what to put in my small travel case. Just a few days before, the Lord told me to buy a bottle of Vitamin C tablets to put with a plastic bottle of water, my Bible, two loaves of bread, two salami, a flashlight, and a sewing kit.

Vitamin C was not available in stores for regular sale, so it had to be obtained through other means. It was very expensive too. Though it made no sense to me, God told me to take this particular vitamin along. It was a warm, sunny day. In the bright morning light our older children trooped off to school. I planned to see them on their return home. I kept looking at my watch, expecting at any moment to hear someone at the door. Dressed in regular, everyday clothes, I waited for my promised two companions to show up. Aurica set the table for lunch, and then we heard a knock at the door. The first to appear was Josef, a man I had met several times at Christian gatherings. We had never discussed escaping together from Romania, so I knew God had supernaturally sent him. Therefore, I could greet him with full joy. "You've come and I've been waiting for you!" I said. Josef's face lit up. "Praise God," he said. "I feel the same, for God has sent us here." Stefan, the next to appear, was Josef's friend. I had never seen him before, but he too had been sent by God to meet with me on this secret date.

Like me, they were lightly dressed in jacket, slacks, and street shoes. We had no choice but to dress lightly, even in cold weather, for warm clothing was simply not obtainable.

Stefan was a mechanic. Josef was a salesman at a large store. Both had wives and families like me. They too had tried many ways to escape, but their struggles had come to nothing. As with Aurica and me, God had given them strong assurances that He would deliver them in His chosen way and time.

There was no indulging in small talk, as we began to pray soon after their arrival. We had prayed for about a half hour when God said we would have to start walking. Walk? That wasn't much guidance, but we all realized we must do as God said.

Stefan was a little uneasy as the time of our exodus drew near. He thought that he needed to return home first to talk to his wife, maybe he thought for the last time. But as we prayed about it his uneasiness was lifted, and he no longer felt the need for the trip home. Josef was more confident. "I need to go with you," he said to me.

We ate lunch to give our bodies the needed strength, but no one much noticed the food, we were so taken up with God's deliverance so close at hand. Aurica, pregnant with our seventh child, Elijah Junior, moved about the tiny kitchen, setting things away. The children began coming home from school now. The reality of leaving them for an indefinite time struck us very hard. Aurica and I could not hold back our tears.

Then the children wanted to know why we were crying. Aurica told them I was going away. I had done so countless times in my line of work, so they thought it was because of that. "We'll be together soon," I assured them.

We prayed for the last time as a family in Timisoara. As we finished the last prayers, God clearly said, "I have sent angels, and I also send a Light before you." It was about 7:00 p.m. in the evening, beginning to grow dark. I hugged and kissed the children and Aurica for the last time. Somehow God gave us the strength to part. But God had so encouraged me in the spirit that I felt that I could fly over the border on wings on faith without my feet touching the ground!

Stefan, Josef, and I stepped out from the house. There in the street was the Light God had promised—the Light of Deliverance. A pillar, a column of intense, bluish-white light stood about ten meters away. It was indescribably beautiful, hovering a little above the ground, in height about seven feet tall. My breath was taken away by the sheer beauty and wonder of it.

The moment I saw it I heard the unmistakable voice of Jesus the Good Shepherd: *"Fear not, My children, now is the time you have to leave. Follow the Light. Do not look left or right or back, just follow the Light. And go! Where the Light stops, you will stop and pray. Don't be afraid. I will be with you, and will guide you to the right place, and will give you the right direction."*

Stefan could not see the Light of Deliverance, but Josef his friend saw it. That was enough for Stefan, however. We three set off into the dusk, following God's heavenly Light. We felt nothing but joy and peace. If anyone had cut my hand or even shot me, I do not think I would have felt a thing. With our spirits soaring so high, gliding like mighty eagles, we followed the supernatural light, which now left the road and crossed the field behind our house, heading straight across open country.

After a couple of hours, the Light stopped in a big cornfield. We sang songs of praise and prayed. Rain began to fall, though until then the sky was cloudless and clear. We rejoiced when we saw that as an answer to prayer, as God pulled a curtain round about us of dark, thick rain. The rain fell heavier as we followed the Light toward the rendezvous with the KGB's hidden detection system protecting the approaches to the border. It was laid somewhere along the ground, invisible to the eye.

After a while, without any alarm being set off, the Light brought us safely to a field near the border. In the distance we could see a tall, intensely lighted watchtower. Every 500 meters was another such tower, we knew, with fences, soldiers and trained police dogs.

Despite the drenching rain, we felt no discomfort, only great joy in the Lord. The Light moved steadily toward the tower and we followed with rejoicing hearts. A soldier appeared on patrol, accompanied by a police dog. Despite the rain, we had no trouble seeing him in the strong border light that illuminated the entire field between the tower and us. The soldier and his dog were walking from the right of the tower to the left side (and would normally have no difficulty seeing us coming). I entertained no fear, for I kept my eyes on the Light ahead as it continued toward the tower. We followed, despite the soldier and dog coming closer and closer to us.

God had already brought us safely over the KGB detection wire. Thousands of others had not been so fortunate, setting off the alarm, bringing the soldiers with their rifles blazing. Stefan was looking at the soldier. He whispered in my ear, "Elijah, we are finished! They'll catch us!"

Somehow, I kept my eyes on the beautiful Light which outshone the border light. We walked toward the tower. The soldier and dog moved away from us just as we came up to them. We then walked under the tower and still nothing happened to us, despite the guard standing watch just above us. Beyond the tower, we realized that we were now across the line into Yugoslavia, the doorstep of freedom for Romanian refugees.

God had done it! With our own eyes we had seen the impossible happening, the most stupendous event of our lives. Detection wire, tower light and guard, roving guard and dog—like Pharaoh they sank defeated into the waters of the Red Sea and could do us no longer any harm whatsoever! We were now in Yugoslavia, and all three of us had just seen God Almighty delivering us just like He had delivered Moses and the people of Israel with great signs and wonders. We were witnesses. We saw how he had taken control over the alarm system, the soldiers, the dog, over the very forces of nature—WE WERE FREE! Set free, I must tell everyone I meet, not by our own hand or sword, not even by luck. No, we walked across the Romanian border as if it had not been there and everything that could possibly have harmed us was completely neutralized. No human being could have done what we did and lived to tell about it. That feat took a God who does impossible things. And this indescribably awesome God was with us still, when we came to face many dangerous or impossible situations in Yugoslavia.

Chapter 13: "Three Jonahs"

Following the Light of Deliverance into Yugoslavia, we felt exhilarated by the sense of new freedom; yet hundreds of kilometers of hostile and unknown terrain still lay between us and true liberty in Italy and Austria. How we ached to stop and rejoice after the crossed the border! But the Light kept moving on ahead in the pouring rain. And so did we.

Finally, it stopped! We could contain our joy no longer. "Hallelujah!" "Praise the Lord!" Jesus, thank you!" "Glory to God!" We couldn't stop crying out praises such as these for some time. In the midst of a field of sunflowers, we hugged each other and danced about like King David before the Ark of God. It was ten minutes before midnight when we halted with the column of Light. In a few minutes it would be October 10. Now we knew exactly how the ancient Israelites felt as they watched the thundering waves churn up broken spears, dead bodies, and smashed chariots from Pharaoh's demolished, drowned army where Hebrew feet had just trod. Jumbled together with such debris were no doubt all the iron foot shackles, neck collars, and work-gang chains Pharaoh intended to put back on the Israelites (those who survived the slaughter, that is)—but the God of Israel had other plans for His people!

The joy in our hearts was beyond full expression! But Jesus our Commander-in-Chief cautioned us with a word: "Already you have crossed the border. But you must be careful. You are still in a dangerous place." Realizing we needed to keep our voices low, we set off after the again moving Light. Without knowledge or any map of the country, we had only to pray as previously instructed and God always told us what to do. Whenever we approached danger, God faithfully warned us.

We walked all that night and into the morning, stopping only when the Light, always in front of us, paused. Later we would learn that we had passed straight through the most dangerous part of Yugoslavia, Serbia, containing the capital Belgrade, the central government, and the greatest concentration of Yugoslavia's police and soldiers. We did not stop walking until the night of October 10th, being led through open countryside away from roads. After a time, we were led along country lanes, and later a highway. Keeping away from people, we gleaned potatoes, apples, and corn from the fields, which we cooked over campfires. The weather turned mild, without rain or wind.

In the two weeks it took for us to reach Zagreb, a large city and rail center, we found God's guidance at every point. Yet we sometimes missed His perfect direction temporarily by complaining or stubbornly going our own way. Once we came to a big river at night. We had to cross, but how? Stefan took a tree branch and went along the riverbank, testing the waters. "We'll never make it across!" he cried. He found the river far too deep and turbulent. "But, my friend," I objected, "the Light stopped over here. We have to cross right here."

Stefan keep insisting though the river was too deep to ford. We would all be drowned. Yet when we went into the water where the column of Light stopped we found we could walk across without any difficulty. Where Stefan tested the water, it was impossible. But the Light led us to the exact place where the water proved to be only a foot or so deep all the way across to the opposite bank.

Again, in the mountains a similar problem developed. We spent days vainly circling the same mountain peak, unable to cross a precipitous gorge. Cold, hungry and tired, we finally gave up and prayed for guidance. It was early in the morning, close to daybreak. In the dawning light we finished our prayers and looked up. It was then we saw God's answer had been within easy reach the whole time we spent circling the mountain. A short distance away was a manually operated cable car!

We walked into Zagreb at night and found ourselves in the railyards. Around us stretched long lines of boxcars. Some boxcars held sheep, and we naturally felt that it would be nice and warm inside with the sheep, but God told us not to get in any boxcar with sheep, and to walk farther on. We found a boxcar loaded with lumber. God told us to take it, which meant that no longer could we depend on the Light of Deliverance for safety and guidance. At the same time, He said we, like Jonah, would be in that boxcar for three days and three nights. We climbed up into the boxcar, which was roofless and filled with boards, of the type used for fences. Under the lumber, we hollowed out a little den and settled down to wait for God's deliverance. Presently the train started down the tracks. All through the night it moved, stopped, and moved again, adding new cars and letting others off. Back and forth our boxcar was shunted, and we never could tell where we were being taken.

"Where will the train take us?" Stefan kept asking above the clacking roar of the moving cars. "Maybe it's taking us back into Romania, or Hungary!" Well, Romania was certain death, and Hungary was communist too, and certainly no refuge for us, but I said, "Praise God! Jesus is the Engineer of this train. He knows where we are going!" Boom, boom! Our boxcar crashed back and forth against its couplings. We had no food or water left. And without water the highly spiced and salted salami was inedible. Huddling together under a load of lumber was extremely uncomfortable. We did not dare look out and so had to ride in the dark, hour after hour.

The Lord had told me to bring Vitamin C. This vitamin, we now discovered, helped us to bear our terrible thirst. We each took a tablet every hour.

The second day we heard voices outside the boxcar. The voice sounded suspiciously Yugoslavian—but we could not be sure. Stefan whispered he wanted to climb out and see, but we would not let him because of the danger. Without a single look at the country, we rode the boxcar farther and farther into the unknown countryside.

The train finally halted. We heard police coming to check the boxcars for stowaway refugees, so we knew it was some border crossing. The border guard walked across the roofless, loaded boxcars, stepping right over our heads. He had a trained dog, for we heard him give his dog a command. Yet the dog failed to scent us, and they went on to inspect the other boxcars.

The train moved on into a different country that we could only hope was free and non-communist. We stopped eventually and heard someone speaking a language that sounded like—Italian? We could not be sure, since we heard only a few words, so we remained in our hiding place. At 5 o'clock the next morning the train stopped. It was the end of the allotted time, the three days and three nights. Our Jonah-like ordeal had passed. We were free to climb out of the boxcar, though we still did not know where on earth we had landed!

Dazed by the experience of hiding so long in the dark, we pulled the boards away from overhead and climbed out into the light where living people lived. Like men who had lain in a grave for three days, we could barely move our cramped muscles and somehow got down to the ground. We had to support one another, we were so weak and floppy. All we could see were trains, so we started walking as best we could. Then we came to a water pump. No one was around to prevent us, so we drank great gulps and washed our hands and faces. Walking a little farther, we saw the sign: "VENICE TRAIN STATION."

Hallelujah! This was the complete and full deliverance promised us! God had brought us through every hazard and snare and trial by His amazing grace and power! Now, glorious Lord, may your Name be praised in all the earth for the great things you did for us! Amen

Chapter 14: "No Passport but Jesus"

At the Venice train station, we were able to communicate with people, using Romanian, for Romanian and Italian are closely related languages. We hurried into the streets, wide-eyed as children. What wonders! Shops and stores over-flowing everywhere with food and luxury goods, the like of which we never saw in our homeland, and vehicles crowded the streets, not the bicycles and everyone else on foot! Best of all, we breathed a perfume in the air that was freedom. Freedom! Our bodies tingled with a vibrant sensation that newly freed men must all feel. Colors were so bright and smiles so warming in this free country, the very pavement made our feet want to dance!

Although lacking money, we still had on us the two, expensive salamis God told me to take. These sold without difficulty, gaining us enough currency for haircuts, stamps, and postcards. We wrote our wives and families that we had just arrived safely in Venice, Italy. I also wrote Aurica that we would surely be together soon, as God had promised.

It was sheer bliss to have a shave and haircut and freshen up for the journey to the refugee camp. After our postcards were mailed we went to a policeman and told him we were Romanian refugees seeking asylum. The friendly officer took us to the nearest police station. There we were fingerprinted and questioned, for they had to determine if we were truly refugees and not communist spies or KGB agents. The police were amazed by our story. "That's a miracle!" they exclaimed. They told us that groups of people tried to escape from Romania and were always caught in Yugoslavia and sent back. This was the first time they had received three refugees in one group who had escaped from Romania via Yugoslavia.

After giving us some things for our stay in Italy, they transported us by train to the refugee center outside Trieste. Before I even reached the camp, God spoke to me about leaving Italy for neighboring Austria. I went to the refugee center, however, expecting God to work out my itinerary. A car was waiting at the train station and took us to the big refugee camp. It was one of the camps for people who have fled communist lands. Austria, Germany, Italy, and now Yugoslavia operate refugee camps for thousands of people seeking freedom in the West.

On October 26th, we arrived in Venice and were taken to a camp outside Trieste. We were expected to remain a minimum of three days, and could depart only if we had passports and visas for travel to other countries.

The Lord again spoke to me about leaving the camp. I was to leave on the third day. Meanwhile, Stefan, Josef and I shared with others at the camp our escape story showing God's miraculous deliverance. They all listened attentively, though most had not gained their freedom like us by trekking out of a communist country on foot. Highly privileged, card-carrying communists traveling abroad as tourists, they had thrown their precious cards away the moment they arrived in a free country.

One of them was George, a well-paid engineer of Romania. He believed in Jesus as Lord and Savior when he heard our story. George immediately attached himself to me, and he was not put off when I told him God was sending me to Austria in a couple days. "I want to go with you!" he insisted, though he knew I had no money and passport for the trip. "I don't want to go alone, Elijah," George kept saying to me. "If you go, I want to go with you." George had a passport. He also had money for his travel expenses. I had no passport and no money. "I have to go," I replied, and so we set out from the camp in the evening of the third day.

I had to explain to Stefan and Josef that the Lord had decided to send me to Austria without them. But I told them that I would return for them or send help in some way (though, later, they chose to accept another man's help instead).

At the train station George bought both our tickets, one-way fares to Vienna. After buying the tickets, he turned to me. "Elijah, I have bought the tickets, but what will you do? You have no passport." I could see that he was a little afraid and was having second thoughts about our journey. "God will take care of that," I replied.

We walked to our compartment on the train and took seats with three other people. They knew each other. Two were stylish young men. The third was a lady doctor. They all spoke Romanian.

"Oh, are you Romanian too?" cried George in happy surprise.

George was so delighted that he quickly told them the details of my story, the miracle of the border crossing and escape...and the fact that I had no passport. "Just look at this man here!" he exclaimed, pointing to me. "He and two friends escaped a few days ago from Romania in a wonderful way, delivered by God. He is truly trusting God! He doesn't even have a passport, but God protects him!"

The lady was a doctor of psychology. She balked immediately and could not believe such a tale. "Oh, that's hard to believe," she shrugged, "since he doesn't have a passport." Then the seriousness of my situation struck her. She looked closely at me. Her sophisticated expression turned to anxiety for my safety. "How can you be here on this train without a passport?" she demanded.

I did not respond at once. She grew all the more anxious. "What are you doing here?" she insisted. The lady doctor and I were seated on opposite sides by the window, so I gazed directly at her. "Praise God," I said with a smile. "I spoke with God, and God told me to be here."

George, forgotten in the turn of conversation, stared at us and was speechless. Perhaps he was waiting to see what dreadful thing was going to happen to me now, due to my lack of a passport. The lady psychologist was still exasperated. She looked with pity on me. "How can you claim to speak with God?" she asked cynically. She shifted uncomfortably on the seat. "I believe in God. I pray. But how can you say that you speak with God? I believe you have a mental problem." She glanced around the compartment, but the two young men seemed to believe my story and were not offering her support in her diagnosis.

But I knew her concerns, at face value, were valid. As a believer in God, maybe once a year at Easter she went to church. But I also knew that there is a big difference between those who merely believe in God's existence and those who "believe God" for the sustaining of their very lives...those who wholeheartedly follow Him.

The lady turned to me with a common question. "What kind of church, what denomination are you affiliated with? For you say you speak with God." For a moment it seemed she had forgotten her concern for my mental condition The mention of speaking with God had obviously upset her, so I turned to her again with the truth. "Yes, we can speak with God," I answered. "We can do it because we are God's children."

I left her to think about this and prayed silently. As I was praying the Lord spoke to my heart. "Fear not, my son. I am with you, and I intend to show these people my power." Immediately I saw fleecy white clouds cover me with invisibility. The vision was a great encouragement at that moment, for we all knew the border police were coming to check our passports.

I spoke to the lady doctor. "God has said that He will protect me. The police will not be able to see me. By that miracle you will see God's mighty power, for God intends to touch your hearts." The lady stared, her mouth open, but she quickly recovered her dignity. "You are crazy!" she huffed. "I don't see how you can speak with God. I never heard of people who could do that!"

Yes, when we pray we speak with Him," I explained. "He is our Father, and in Him I trust. He is my protector. He is everything to me."

The lady turned aside to the others, remembering my passport problem. Could I not hide under the seats? they wondered. But they looked beneath and saw that a heating system took up all the space under the two seats. The train was already moving. The conductor entered the compartment and took our tickets. The air grew thick with tension. Everyone around me was afraid to speak. No one said a word as the conductor went out and two policemen entered. As they methodically checked passports, I just kept praying silently, my head bowed. The policemen never asked me for a passport, though they checked everyone else in the compartment. They asked if we had anything to declare for Customs charges. No one offered to declare items, so they shut the door and left us.

The moment they were gone the lady threw up her hands. "My goodness, what happened?" she cried out. She turned to me. "I don't understand!" What kind of faith, what kind of religion, what denomination are you anyway?" George and the two young men were all rejoicing, but I had to answer the lady's burning questions.

"I love Jesus, He is my Redeemer," I explained, for I always try to avoid denominational fence-building. "That's exactly what God wanted to do, to show you His great power and grace. I do believe God is planning to save your soul as well." The lady was so struck by such a thought that she became quiet.

The express train sped rapidly toward the Austrian border. We all knew there would be another confrontation with the police who checked passports on the Austrian side. We waited, as the atmosphere in the compartment grew charged with suspense and deathly quiet. Austrian police entered. "Pass Kontrol, bitte," one said briskly in German. Everyone else held up passports, while I sat as before praying silently, my head bowed.

Again, I was totally ignored by the police. They closed the door. The moment they were gone the woman jumped up from her seat. "Praise the Lord!" she cried. "Praise the Lord!" One of the young men sprang up to stop her shouting. "Please be quiet!" he pleaded. "The police could hear you and come back and ask what is happening here." But the lady doctor was not to be deterred by his fears or common sense. Great joy showed on her face. "That's God!" she declared authoritatively. "Please tell us about your faith."

I could see her heart had indeed been touched to the depths. The two young men were also affected. They now revealed their own secret: neither had a visa to enter Germany where they were going to immigrate. "Please pray for us," they implored.

First, I saw their greater need. I explained a portion of scripture, Romans 10: 9-10, and led them in prayer, so that they might receive forgiveness of their sins and confess Jesus as their newfound Lord and Savior. They all, the two young men and the lady doctor, became believers before the train reached our destination. As we drew near to Vienna, I received a vision concerning their lack of visas (for they were terribly afraid they would be turned back at the border). I told them God had revealed that the police would merely glance at their unopened passports at the border but would not check them for the necessary visas. Later they wrote to me to report that it happened exactly as God had shown in the vision.

The train slowed to a stop at the station in Vienna with our compartment full of rejoicing Romanians.

Chapter 15: "Goose Chase in Germany"

George and I had no time in Vienna for enjoying tours of the grandly styled city of Mozart and Strauss. I needed to contact my longtime friend, Siegmund, who headed a gospel and literature mission to communist nations. Unfortunately, I had only the number of his post office box and not his home address. We left our hotel near the train station and walked across town and to the post office where Siegmund picked up his mail. We trudged into the post office, only to be confronted by a suspicious clerk who refused to give out Siegmund's home address. So, I wrote a brief word and left it in his box.

George and I returned to the hotel to wait for Siegmund to contact us there. Several days passed with no sign of my friend. I heard God tell me to go to the refugee camp outside Vienna. I was about to go, but George had another idea. The camps in Germany were so much better than Austrian camps, he kept insisting. He also said that he had friends and contacts in Germany who would surely help us in our plans. I listened to George and, against my better judgment, turned toward Germany.

We took a train to Salzburg on the border of West Germany. George believed it was a simple matter to hop over the border on foot, waltz around the German patrols, and skip straight to the nearest refugee camp. We both had heard the authorities were hard on those they caught; but once a refugee reached a camp he was allowed to stay on in the country.

We set out from Salzburg on foot. It was night, and in the dark we heard a German patrol whistling a little tune as he approached. Hiding behind trees, we waited until he passed merrily on his way. When he was out of earshot we crossed the border into Germany. How easy!

Bavaria is extremely picturesque, with forests, lakes, castles on islands, and mountain peaks, but it was so dark when we crossed over we wandered about and bumped against trees, hopelessly lost. At last we came to a road, but first I had to warn George about what God had shown me. Though ordinarily a brave and intelligent man, George was not accustomed to a refugee's life. He did not know what to say or do in really difficult circumstances. "George," I said, "God told me if you do anything wrong, we have to pay the price, so please be careful about what you say or do."

"I'm tired," was his response. "That's just the way it is," I replied. "We have to walk."

We were standing now by a road and could follow it to some town or village. But a car approached. George immediately attempted to stop the vehicle, expecting a nice ride to the nearest town. Stop, they did. But, alas, it was the police! In a flash we had to high-tail it into the woods, with the police hot on our trail. But they also acted on impulse, leaving their dog behind in the car. So, they had to run back to get the dog before resuming the chase. George and I came to a wide and deep river. We foolishly plunged in and somehow made it to the other shore. I had to drag poor George out onto the riverbank. Then we continued in our soggy shoes and clothes and came to an open gas station.

An attendant was there on duty despite the late hour, so I used the German I had learned from my German father to ask directions to the nearest train station. The man told us it was in Petting Bitting, only three or four kilometers away.

We found the little, cozy, warm train depot. Inside we dried ourselves off by the heat registers. Feeling better, George engaged the station clerk in a detailed account about my escape from Romania, adding candidly that we were Romanian refugees.

Hearing this, my heart immediately sank into my shoes. The agent called the police. In two minutes, they arrived at the station and arrested us, since we were illegal immigrants without visas. Thoroughly exhausted, and knowing it was futile to resist, we were taken to jail. Our reception, as we had been forewarned, was rough. The Germans had no particular liking for illegal aliens. George was upset by the treatment we received. He had never been in jail before. "George," I reminded my friend, "I told you not to make any mistake."

But I knew my own mistake: failing to obey God's explicit command to go to the Austrian camp instead of trying to sneak in Germany's back door. Now we both had to suffer the consequences of George's impulsiveness and my own disobedient agreement in following him. The police already had a large group of illegal Yugoslavians on their hands. We were put with them, then questioned.

I told the police everything from start to finish, taking care not to deviate or change my story in any way. I was completely honest. George, I learned, did not know how to keep to the facts. His story swerved first one way and then another as he was being questioned. The police soon grew upset with him, while they became friendlier toward me. When asked to declare any money, I told them the truth: none. George promptly said the same. But soon he was in big trouble, for a small fortune was discovered hidden in his shoe.

Angry over George's lying, the police called in a translator, an old German who had lived many years in Romania. We were questioned again. My story held at all points. George's story fell apart. When we were alone, I warned George that he was making things worse for himself by not being straightforward with the police. But he became very upset. He was petrified that they would send him back to Romania (a distinct possibility because of his lies).

Concerned for his safety, I prayed for him. George was so deeply affected by the possibility of forced return to Romania, where he would be imprisoned and possibly executed, his hair color changed overnight!

I had previously heard of such cases of extreme stress, but still it amazed me to see George's hair turn white.

Two weeks after our arrest, the questioning was concluded. The police put us all in a big, black van. Twenty Yugoslavians and two Romanians were being taken SOMEWHERE, but the Yugoslavians acted as though they knew everything. On the way to the border they kept prodding George, saying that he was being sent back to Yugoslavia, and thence to the lion's den of Romania. Not knowing that they were only trying to scare him, George fell to their tactics. George was completely overcome with the fearful prospect of returning to Romania and the potential consequences.

"We're all being sent back to Yugoslavia," they said to George, "and when you get to our country the police will boot you back to Romania!" George believed every terrible word and broke down completely. He became so sick to his stomach he could not even control his bodily functions. It is not nice to say, but the truth is poor George couldn't help making a mess in his pants. Soon his devilish tormenters, who had achieved their cruel aim, were laughing and trying to move away from my wretched friend in the crowded vehicle.

The van suddenly stopped. George and I were called out. Leaving us on the road to the local prison, the van sped off. Dazed and surprised, George looked at the nearby Austrian prison and realized God had granted mercy, despite the mess he had made of his testimony. Within minutes, he perked up and looked much improved in his expression, if not in hair color and body.

"Don't be afraid, we won't be sending you back to Romania," the prison authorities assured us. "But we must ask why you two didn't go to the refugee camp here in Austria when you first arrived?" "Why, I was foolish!" I replied. "God said to go to the refugee camp, but I ignored my better judgment, choosing Germany instead."

It had been a hard lesson, but we had both learned something. The stay in the Austrian prison lasted two weeks, but they treated us very well. Then we were taken to the refugee camp where we should have gone in the first place.

Chapter 16: "The Senator's Golden Key"

Austria's refugee camp was large and crowded. The director was hard-pressed, for each refugee took considerable time to process. Everyone knew from the start that one would be in the camp at least two weeks before being set free. George and I were given beds in a communal room shared with about twenty-five people. One night as I slept I had a delightful dream by which God imparted a word. I told George about it in the morning. I had seen a lovely, clear-running river. Siegmund and I were in a boat fishing.

George could not see it. We had tried contacting Siegmund before the Germany caper, and not one word from him since. "Oh, not that fellow!" he sniffed. "He has forgotten you. He doesn't respond to your note. I bet he hasn't the slightest concern for your welfare." "But George," I objected, "according to this dream I feel very sure that I will be set free this very day." "Impossible!" George laughed. "You have to wait for the interview just like everyone else, and there are lots and lots of people here ahead of us. Everyone says..."

People around us had been listening to George's remarks, so I turned to relate the dream and its meaning to them, since they already knew our escape story and the details of God's deliverance. Some had believed in Jesus after hearing our story, but this they could not swallow. They all had been waiting longer than we had for the camp director's interview. So, they all laughed together with George as we walked to the dining hall for breakfast.

I still believe I'll be set free today," I told them "Maybe I have interpreted it wrongly, but according to the dream I'm supposed to be out of here today." After a meal it was the custom to walk leisurely down a huge hallway for exercise. George and I were strolling along when someone at the window called out that the camp director was coming to our building (the hallway was on the second floor and looked out on the main entrance).

I went to look and saw the director. There was a man with him. In a few minutes, the director and his companion found me. I recognized the other man, of course. It was Siegmund! He was happy and astonished to see me. "You are supposed to be dead at the border!" he exclaimed. Then he explained what had happened to him. He had been away on a trip to America. He was just now getting to read his mail. He read my note and went to the hotel at once. Failing to find us, he read the long list of refugees at the camp and discovered my name. What perfect timing God has in getting His children together! He allowed time for George and me to learn our lesson, then arranged for Siegmund and me to be reunited like this. God is good!

As a friend of the director, Siegmund got me an interview on the spot. I was asked a few questions in the main office, and the director said to come back later at my convenience for the remaining questions. Free to go with Siegmund, I spoke to George before departing. My friend was very grieved that he could not go. I asked the director for him, but was told that he could not let George go just yet; his story changed too many times back in Germany. "He will have to be interviewed a long time before we can let him go."

Siegmund arranged lodgings for me, and I began work at the mission, which supplied Bibles and literature to Christians in communist countries in Eastern Europe. As soon as possible I wrote and sent money, food and other things to Aurica and the family. A mission worker came one day from visiting the refugee camp at Trieste, Italy. He told me he was at the camp looking for me. He found Josef and Stefan instead, who informed him of my going on to Vienna with George. They decided to accept his offer of help rather than wait for what I could do. Both Stefan and Josef now reside in Europe with their families.

There was plenty of work at the mission with Siegmund and his brave and dedicated cohorts, but I knew God was calling me to go to America. If I did not go there before two years, the law would prevent me from immigrating. So, I left Siegmund and the mission and flew to Los Angeles, finding a place to stay with a fellow Romanian.

Trusting God to work out the reunion of my family, I called Aurica and reassured her of God's intention to bring us together in America soon. It was February 3rd, 1976 (over a year since the escape) when I settled in Los Angeles, and things still looked hopeless to Aurica. I cried to God constantly for Aurica and the children. Sometimes Aurica was allowed to telephone out and speak to her "runaway criminal" of a husband. One time when she called she was crying. "The police in Bucharest said that there is no way I could ever get a passport," she lamented. She even thought that she might not be able to force herself to face the authorities again with the passport request.

But God had given me a word that He was going to favor us, according to I Samuel 2:26. "I know God will finish this work He has started," I told her. "We will soon be together as He promised. Be joyful and trust in..." Our connection was cut, but not before she had heard God's wonderful promise. I continued to pray for my family's release, while working nights at various jobs and ministering to Romanian people during the day.

At this time God gave me an unusual dream. In the dream there was a guide to lead me. We came upon a distinguished, older gentleman. The guide told me that the man was Henry M. Jackson, a United States Senator from the State of Washington. I saw the Congressman holding a golden key in his hand.

The guide explained that this was the key the Senator would use to gain my family's release. I awoke and was given a vision that repeated exactly what I had seen in the dream—a divine doubling that, as Joseph told Pharaoh, meant that God would certainly do what He had promised, and quickly!

"And for that the dream was doubled unto Pharaoh twice; it is because the thing is established by God, and God will shortly bring it to pass." (Genesis 41:32) But Senator Jackson was completely unknown to me. I had never even heard his name before. So, I asked my Romanian friend. He had been in America for a while and was well-acquainted with the Senator's name and reputation. "He's very powerful in Congress," he said. "And he is a compassionate man, a great help to refugees."

My friend found Senator Jackson's Washington, D. C. address, and I wrote a letter relating the dream I had of him and gave a few details of my family's situation. Senator Jackson wrote back promising to do as much as possible to gain my family's release. I sent a second letter giving more details of my wife's difficult situation, and the Senator's second response made my heart leap for joy. "I was really impressed with your testimony about how you left Romania, and with your dream about me," he wrote. "I am sure that next week your family will receive the passport."

As my friend read the letter to me, I was praising God. I was even more joyful when Aurica called a few days later. She was crying again, but this time with tears of joy. "I don't know what happened," she exclaimed, "but I just picked up our passports. The police came to the house and told me to take the first train to Bucharest at once!" So she rushed to the capital, and at the government passport bureau a high-ranking official handed her a passport. "Here is your passport," he told her. "Get out of the country as soon as possible!"

Aurica was ready. The suitcases were packed. The government gave her 2,000 lei (or about $20.00) for our house, which was just enough to cover the taxi fare from the Vienna train station to the refugee camp. The furnishings and our belongings were given to the poor. Off she went, taking our seven children (for Elijah Jr. had been born after my escape) by train to Austria. Rejoicing over what God had accomplished, I still had a high hurdle to overcome. How was I to get a passport to meet Aurica in Austria? U.S. law said that I could receive a passport to travel from America only after two years residence in the country. If before that time I left the U.S. my ticket might as well be one-way.

After submitting this to God in prayer, I went to the U.S. Immigration Department in Los Angeles. "Impossible," responded a clerk to my request. I asked to see the director. Trembling in my shoes, I explained to the director my family's difficult status as refugees and my need to meet my wife Aurica and our seven children at the camp in Austria. "Go to the office downstairs," he said. "I promise that they will give you what you ask for there."

It was exactly as he promised. The somewhat rattled clerks issued me a White Passport, the first of that color I had ever seen. I flew at once to Vienna. At the refugee camp the director met me. He was astonished to see me back so soon. "Why did you come back?" he cried. "You made a big mistake! Now you won't be able to return to America."

I showed him the special White Passport. He too had never seen one and asked to examine it. I went to see Aurica and the children, for they had just eaten a meal and were resting in their quarters. I found them and we all rushed into each other's arms. There was crying and rejoicing all that night and morning. Since the White Passport was good for a year, we could spend the summer resting and enjoying family life together again after a lapse of two long years.

God had finished what he had started so long ago in Romania. Everything came to pass despite all the efforts of Romanian government officials and police! And with my unique White Passport, we could all fly to America, to begin life anew and serve God as He had called us to do.

Finally rested, we took leave of Vienna. Though we embarked on a jet airliner, we really flew to our new life on the great, soaring wings of God's grace.

Chapter 17: "Dark Threads"

In December 1976, we arrived in the United States. A Christian friend had rented a brand-new house for us in Anaheim, a suburb of Los Angeles. Aurica and the children stepped into their new American home. They looked wide-eyed at the four bedrooms, two baths, the living room and large kitchen. It was the kitchen appliances that took their breath away. The refrigerator was filled with food, and next to it gleamed a stove Aurica must have thought dropped from heaven. Furniture filled the house. We toured each room and continually broke out in praise and thanks to God.

But our schedule did not leave us much time for wandering awestruck about the lovely home and garden. God raised up a church, the Romanian Apostolic Church in Santa Fe Springs, which I pastored. Each year afterwards God led me to start another new church—so that days were taken up completely in church ministry.

Nights I spent working as an office cleaner. Our family was large, compared with most American households, but with God's help we were able to afford the payment of rent and a car, enjoying most of the usual conveniences of life in America. I found a job as a custodian at a large church and church-school, Prince of Peace Lutheran Church, Costa Mesa, California. I also took work as a field manager on a commercial farm outside Los Angeles. The time passed swiftly for us. Three more children were to be born to us, all full-fledged Americans! And our ministry in churches was blessed and extended, for I was asked to speak in many parts of the country and even on a nationwide, Christian television network.

But aside from the stresses of enemy attack and our great deliverance from Romania, Aurica and I and our family experienced the most serious crises of our lives in this "City of Angels," Los Angeles.

First, we had some mishaps with our "newest" American—our son Benjamin. The worst incident with Benjamin occurred when the truck we used on the farm started moving accidentally and rolled over Benjamin, crushing his head nearly flat. Rushed by ambulance to Bakersfield Hospital, Benjamin experienced a miraculous healing. We will never forget the look of amazement on the face of the doctor who had seen the first X-rays. "Incredible!" he said to us several hours after admitting Benjamin. "That's just incredible! From the time we took the first X-rays three hours ago, his head has returned to normal! I really don't know what as happened. There doesn't even seem to be any brain damage."

In these and other incidents with Benjamin, we all saw God's power, care, mercy and healing evidenced dramatically. But shortly we would experience God's mercy in a completely different way. At the start of the same year, I was fasting and praying for direction from the Lord. I still had no conception of the great thing God was soon to accomplish in our midst. Aurica and I had received a word about God's plan to do something with our family. But just because God said that He was going to do something, that was no cause, as we saw it, to be alarmed.

In March the warning signs grew more disturbing. Elijah Jr. had two dreams. He was in a park filled with flowers and had played with angels. In the next dream he saw himself run over by a large bull. He was so upset about the bull that Aurica and I had to pray with him before he finally settled down and slept. A little boy's nightmares can be easily dismissed, but about that time our daughter, Lidia, came to us with a startling dream. She had seen Jesus standing in our garden. Jesus told her that He was going to pick one of our flowers, a rose rare and sweet. Although we could plainly see something was about to happen, we put the worst possibilities out of mind. Elijah Jr. was just too lively a boy for us to worry about his health.

A Romanian family was staying with us, sponsored by us for immigration, so there were seventeen children in the house who needed to be fed and clothed. To keep up with their appetites took a lot of food, so it was not surprising that Aurica and I were away at the store when God said to me: "Return home immediately!" Feeling a heavy sense of foreboding, I turned to Aurica and forgot all about preparations for dinner. "We need to go home at once," I told my wife. "I feel something has happened!"

It was about 5:00 PM when we rushed through the door to find the police waiting for us. They said that they had been trying to reach us by telephone. Little Elijah Jr., they said, was in the hospital. Weeping and praying, we rushed to the Emergency Room and learned he had been struck down by a car while crossing a street. He had permission to go to our neighborhood park with the older children. But the older ones wanted to go to another park further away, which meant crossing the very busy Beach Boulevard. All the children made it safely across to the second park, but when they were returning home a car ran over little Elijah.

The doctors would not let us see him. Aurica and I could not sit in the waiting room any longer without seeing our boy, so I quickly looked up a telephone number. I knew a doctor who was a surgeon, and I called him from the hospital. He came right over to see if he could be of help I was called in to the operating room. But the sight of my son's blood and all the doctors and nurses huddled over that precious little form drove me out into the hall weeping.

Aurica and I prayed and wept, prayed and wept, until I said to her that I could pray no more. It was in God's hands, I realized. Then I saw, distinctly, a circle of angels rising above us and above the hospital, lifting little Elijah Jr. toward heaven. Little by little, the circle of angels and our son ascended and finally disappeared. Having seen this, I was quiet before the Lord. Forty minutes later, our doctor-friend came out of the operating room. "He is gone," he said.

Aurica and I heard his words but we could not take them in. When we turned to go home, I argued with God all the way. Yet God pierced through the dark grief. "Why are you crying?" the Lord asked. "You are crying because I took My child home to Me? This was My plan. I have much more about this to show you later, and then you will understand."

After hearing the Lord's reproof, I realized it was fruitless to argue with Him. His ways are perfect, though we may not understand them right away. In a short time, we began to see that God had prepared a great blessing to come from the seeming tragedy of little Elijah Jr.'s death. It gradually unfolded like a gleaming pattern of silver threads out of the dark tapestry of our sorrow and loss. Several hundred people attended the funeral service. They were so touched by the message given on that day that at least twenty people re-dedicated their hearts and lives to the service of the Lord. Others received Jesus as Lord and Savior and were saved, born-again as new Christians!

We were not able to speak with the poor woman who had driven the car that struck down our little son. Police would not give out her address, fearing retaliation. Nevertheless, we prayed for her. Several years passed. I was at the airport talking with other passengers waiting for a flight in Dallas, Texas, when the conversation turned to the accident. I told the people around me how, in the various lives touched by God at the funeral service, good had come out of seeming evil. A woman listening to me responded with a story of her own. She began telling of her daughter-in-law, who lived in Garden Grove (next to Anaheim where we lived) and who had run over and killed a Romanian boy.

I listened with absolute amazement as she told how her daughter-in-law sat for weeks after the accident in numbness and despair at home, fearing another accident if she got behind the wheel again. Finally, one day as she was watching a Christian television program, she heard the Good News about forgiveness of sins and salvation in Jesus Christ. That was all she needed to set her free. It was then that she gave her heart to the Lord Jesus. When she told her family, all eight, including her mother-in-law telling me the story, believed in Jesus as their Lord.

Later, I told this to my family, and they too were overjoyed. The way it touched our hearts is indescribable, for we greatly missed little Elijah Jr.

> *God weaves a tapestry 'midst sin and strife*
> *He takes the pain and loss, dark threads of life,*
> *and someday, when we view His face,*
> *we'll see the golden pattern—Grace!*

Chapter 18: "Consider the Ravens"

It is not easy for an immigrant family to adjust and earn its way in completely different circumstances in America, but God helped us in every way. Sometimes God will bless through unusual means. We learned this as we were driving home from a trip. We were still about 120 miles from Los Angeles when I heard two, distinct voices, in a fierce tug-of-war.

"I'm going to kill him!" said one voice out of "nowhere." "No, I won't let you!" countered another voice from the same dimension. Four of the children with me were asleep, but Lidia was awake. I told her what I had heard, and together we prayed. God spoke to us: "The Enemy wants to harm you on this trip, but I will be your protection!"

Suddenly, the car seemed to explode. Hurtled into the air, we flew off the road and crashed. I had some minor cuts on my head that were bleeding, but otherwise I was unhurt, so I helped the children out, one by one. Amazingly, they too were unhurt and could stand, though everyone was very shaken and stunned. The car was totally demolished, together with all our belongings. Police and ambulances arrived, and at first, they could not believe our amazingly good condition after being struck from behind by a runaway truck. They examined us, but it was apparent to them that we were all right though our car was totaled. They decided not to take us to the hospital.

Meanwhile, a woman driving a Cadillac parked and came over to us. "Do you recognize me?" she inquired, looked us over with astonishment. I did. "I'm your neighbor!" she exclaimed.

She offered us a ride to our home. Accepting, we got in and heard her tell the story of her own escape from death. She had been driving behind us when she saw a huge truck about to smash into her from behind. Swerving to one side, she watched in horror as the truck struck and smashed our little car instead. It was a demonstration of God's tender care to find He had prepared a ride for us, through our own next-door neighbor, who drove us home from the terrible accident. Our neighbor wasn't an angel, but close enough! The rest of the journey was filled with rejoicing.

When we did not claim anything through the insurance, the company that represented the trucking firm contacted us. Despite no claim, they gave us a check for $10,000. With that sum we bought an almost new van for ministry to churches, and purchased a house—so we were doubly blessed by what momentarily appeared to be a calamity. God has absolute control over all material things—even in terrible accidents, such the one we experienced!

In 1981 I was returning home from a ministry trip in Europe to my responsibilities in the states. I was confronted one day by angels. "Before you left Romania, didn't you promise to work full-time for the Lord?" they asked. They were right. Though I was still working full-time at night and ministering full-time during the day in various churches, I wasn't exactly trusting God to care for us as He does for the ravens.

As the Lord Jesus said: *"Consider the ravens: for they neither sow nor reap; which neither have storehouse nor barn; and God feedeth them; how much more are ye better than the fowls?"* (Luke 12:24)

Working and ministering as I did was a severe strain, and I had been praying for God to do something. Well, God was saying to me that He who filled our empty diesel tank could also fill a checking account! Jehovah our Provider was opening a door of divine provision for the new things he wanted to do with our lives.

Praying about the matter, we knew that we were to trust God for ALL provision. The angels encouraged me and left me believing that God was going to do that "impossible" thing soon. After all, hadn't ravens fed Elijah in a time of terrible drought and famine? That call to consider the ravens came in 1983. About seven years had passed since we first came to America. After accepting God's total provision, our lives changed drastically.

Unsolicited financial support began pouring in by mail soon after the angels' visit. Strangers were touched by God to send assistance to an unknown Romanian minister. The monthly total grew to the point where I could lay down my custodial job at the Lutheran church. I was enabled to travel more abroad, flying to Europe to witness of my Lord and give aid to the refugees. We were able to send trucks and cars full of necessities into Romania itself.

Due to the gifts from mostly unknown people, the ministry to refugees has grown steadily. Hundreds of refugees have been helped with food, clothing, emergency funds, and (most precious) sponsorship to live in a free country. Wonderfully open to the Gospel, refugees from communist countries take their new faith to the U.S., Canada, and Western European countries. The impact of such vibrant, restored lives, made new through Jesus Christ, is beyond estimating.

Of course, the needs of refugees are immense, asking the utmost of what any country, person, or ministry can provide. But the Lord, the Mighty God of Abraham and the Prophet Elijah, is a great provider! As long as refugees need love and care and the good news of Jesus, we plan to continue with the ministry at the camps, despite harassment by communist agents in the camps and elsewhere, even over in America.

To meet such enormous physical and spiritual needs is very difficult. Some have recently lost all their possessions. Others have lost a beloved husband, a wife, or a child in an escape over the border. I can only give them the loving God who had delivered us through similar hardships and tragedies, a loving God who both protect and provides in impossible circumstances.

Romania itself is experiencing a test, a challenge to her very survival as a nation. Driven to the brink by the insane, self-destructive programs of the communist dictator and his government, Romania has been called a second Ethiopia by commentators in the media. Embarrassed by the extreme food shortages, the authorities turn back our emergency food trucks at times, but we try again later and God gets us through to the people who are starving.

Update: Romania has changed politically if not economically, of course, due to the revolution in Romania and the collapse of the Soviet Union; the poverty and the hunger and the lack of necessities continues, despite the return of freedom and a democratic government. Thousands of Romanians, particularly the young, suffer great hardship, and the hardest hit by the economic chaos in Romania may be the orphans, who roam the streets looking for shelter or a crust of bread.

Christians in the U.S. and other countries, not only in Romania, also need to know that there is a God who will stand by us when we find ourselves like the Prophet Elijah at the brook Cherith with nothing whatever in the cupboard.

One incident of God's provision I will always remember. It happened when Aurica and I were still living in Los Angeles and were down to a few dollars. We often had a large refugee family staying with us, and that meant 8 to 10 additional children in addition to the parents. One day I told Aurica that I was going to the store for the umpteenth time, even though I had only enough money left to buy a little bread and milk. Before I could reach the store, an absolute stranger stopped me. He got off his motorcycle and came up to my car window. I assumed that he wanted to ask directions, but instead he reached in, shook my hand, and then disappeared. In my hand was $50.00. Do angels ride motorcycles? After all, this was the "City of Angels"!

As Jesus said, "Consider the ravens..." Yet there may come a test in trusting God for provision. We are told that the brook Cherith dried up BEFORE God spoke to Elijah to move to the village of Zarphath in northern Israel, where God had commanded a widow to feed him. How long did Elijah have to look down at a dusty stream-bed with his stomach growling BEFORE God gave him a word of direction leading him to provision? However long it was, he had to choose to wait on God for provision there at Cherith, and God, we know, did not abandon him because of his demonstrated faith and trust.

Another case of divine provision involved Abraham. Abraham had to build an altar, put his beloved son on it according to God's command, and raise his knife, BEFORE God spoke and spared Isaac's life! BEFORE! Both Elijah and Abraham had to act by faith BEFORE God acted on their behalf. There is the supreme test, for us to trust and obey God even when it looks absolutely impossible that God will come through for us in time to save us. But God is faithful to those who trust and obey, and we know He is not late regarding His promises though He might seem a bit slow at times. He provided a ram in place of Isaac, and Abraham tenderly and gratefully sacrificed the ram on the altar. Abraham then named the place, calling it "YHWH YIREH," which means, "The Lord will provide." From that place-name we derive "Jehovah-Jireh," one of the most beloved names for God. Abraham's altar of supreme faith and supreme sacrifice stood on Mount Moriah, which was no accident, since Mount Moriah became the site of the future Temple.

This Witness of an altar testifies that God is the sole provision for any Holy Spirit-raised ministry or church. It is God alone who provides for His work. If He cares for wild fowls like the ravens, and feeds them when they cry for food, how much more willing is He to care for His children and provide for them!

God provided a single ram for Abraham to sacrifice as a substitute for Isaac. What is one ram anyway? Yet how precious was that ram, because of Who it signified! Back at Beer-sheba in the Negev desert, at Abraham's camp, he had thousands of rams, but they could do him no good on Mount Moriah, even if he could have sent for one in time to spare Isaac. No, God wanted a sacrificial ram that only He could provide. And so, in response to Abraham's obedience and faith, a ram was provided not from Abraham's flocks but God's own hand—the same hand that later, on this very site, provided Jesus the Lamb of God to die and pay the penalty for the sins of all the world.

"Walk in the Light," the testimony of Elijah and his family is ended. But not the truth of it! Let us call upon the Name of the Lord, who is well able to save and deliver. Let us, every one, now chart a new course if need be, but walk in the Light of Deliverance and praise His holy Name, as Psalm 72 says, because everything truly done in His Name will last and be worthwhile doing:

"His Name shall endure forever;
His Name shall continue as long as the sun.
And men shall be blessed in Him;
all nations shall call Him blessed.
Blessed be the Lord God,
the God of Israel,
who only does wondrous things!
And blessed be His glorious name forever!
And let the whole earth
Be filled with His glory.
Amen and Amen."

Don't miss out!

Visit the website below and you can sign up to receive emails whenever R.D. Ginther publishes a new book. There's no charge and no obligation.

https://books2read.com/r/B-A-ABIN-QESLB

BOOKS 2 READ

Connecting independent readers to independent writers.

Also by R.D. Ginther

Becca The Viking & The Heavenly Runes
Becca The Viking & The Heavenly Runes Book 1, Voyage to Lindisfarne
BeccaThe Viking & The Heavenly Runes Book 2 Voyage To Aachen
Becca The Viking & The Heavenly Runes Book 3, Voyage To The Holy Land
Becca The Viking & The Heavenly Runes Book 4 The Voyage Home

RetroStar Chronicles
Anno Stellae 1912
Vision From Space
Anno Stellae 1918
Anno Stellae 1939
Anno Stellae 1967
AnnoStellae 1969
Anno Stellae 1985 & Anno Stellae 1986
Anno Stellae 1987 & Anno Stellae 1994
Anno Stellae 1996 & Anno Stellae 2024
Anno Stellae 2113, Anno Stellae 2145, Anno Stellae 2146, Anno Stellae 2155, Anno Stellae 2165
Anno Stellae 2170
Anno Stellae 2171, Anno Stellae 2251

Anno Stellae 2382, Anno Stellae 2390-91, Anno Stellae 2392
Anno Stellae 2415, Anno Stellae 2433, Anno Stellae 2444
Ano Stellae 2457
Anno Stellae 2456, Anno Stellae 2460, Anno Stellae 4130, Anno
Stellae 4133, Anno Stellae 4146
Chronicle 39 Anno Stellae 5918, Chronicle 40 Anno Stellae 5920,
Chronicle 41 Anno Stellae 5923
Chronicle 42
Chronicle 43, Chronicle 44
Chronicle 45, Chronicle 46
Chronicle 47
Chronicle 48, Chronicle 49, Chronicle 50
Anno Stellae 6700, Anno Stellae 7074, Anno Stellae 7504, Anno
Stellae 7506
Chronicle 55 Anno Stellae 7537, Chronicle 56 Anno Stellae 8033,
Chronicle 57 Anno Stellae 8507
Chronicle 58 Anno Stellae 8732, Chronicle 59 Anno Stellae 10,272
Chronicle 60, Anno Stellae 10,682; Chronicle 61, Anno Stellae
10,999
Chronicle 62
Chronicle Of The Knights Of Axes Of Honor
Anno Stellae 2393
Anno Stellae 4148, Anno Stellae 4149, Anno Stellae 4150, Anno
Stellae 5909, Anno Stellae 5913

Standalone
Walk In The Light
Becca The Viking & The Heavenly Runebook Book 5
The Great Divide
Victorian Christmas Ballads